THE TEACHER'S GUIDE

for

LIVING TO SERVE

A Sixth Grade Character Growth Experience

Jan Black, Author
Steve Hunt and Dave Adamson, Design and Illustration

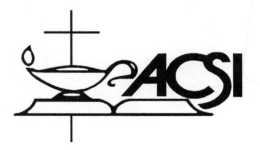 

A Publication of
ASSOCIATION OF CHRISTIAN SCHOOLS INTERNATIONAL
P.O. Box 35097 Colorado Springs, Colorado 80935-3509
Telephone 719/528-6906 † Fax 719/531-0631 † Order Dept 800/367-0798
Website http://www.acsi.org

Teachers,

Throughout the writing of these books, I have sensed a oneness with you, the teacher. I have been where you are. I have stood where you stand and slumped where you slump. Like you, I have been lifted by the love of a child and overwhelmed by the pressures of the job. And perhaps like you, I have wished for materials that would help me help my students in the development of godly character.

This book, and the accompanying student book, is the kind of help I wanted. I hope it is the kind you want also. I have endeavored to present you with a tool for character training that gives you practical help as well as creative options. It is a guide that guides, not dictates. It is one that offers you the meal and serving suggestions, yet lets you choose when and how to serve it.

Focusing on you and your students has been a delight. Studying God as the Source and Strength of character has, as always, been life changing. I am grateful to ACSI for granting me the privilege of this project, and I pray that you who serve on the front lines of Christian education will know that we who serve behind you are cheering you on wholeheartedly.

Thankfully His,

Jan Black
2 Chronicles 16:9

Table of Contents

SP = Student Page
★ = Esther Story
◆ = Servant Story

INTRODUCTION TO CHRISTIAN SCHOOL CURRICULUM

We are pleased to introduce you to Christian School Curriculum, a creative and stimulating program for character development for children. Because your understanding of the curriculum is essential to its best use, we urge you to read the following information carefully. It includes general information for all grade levels, a scope and sequence chart, and specific data pertinent to this book.

CHRISTIAN SCHOOL CURRICULUM: WHAT IT IS MEANT TO BE

A spotlight on the character of God. God is presented as the source and strength of character, and teachers and students are encouraged to respond to Him in worship and admiration.

A multi-level character growth experience. Students will step into the quality being studied by observing behavior, discussing consequences, and participating in activities designed to strengthen their ability to understand and demonstrate each quality.

An integrative tool. The unique nature of each lesson makes it simple for a teacher to integrate character development into a variety of subjects, from language arts to science to Bible.

WHAT CSC INCLUDES

Each grade level includes:

- Nine units of study. Each unit of study includes character traits appropriate in number to each grade level. (See Scope and Sequence chart.)

- Verses to study and/or memorize to reinforce the concepts. These are in addition to a theme passage for grades one through eight.

- Activity pages in the student book which are appealingly designed and illustrated for the mind and heart of a child.

- Parent communicators, beginning with letters home on the lower levels to ideas for teacher contact on the upper levels.

- Bible and everyday examples of each quality. Children learn by watching, and in this curriculum they will watch contemporary and Bible people succeeding, and sometimes failing, in their effort to do right.

- Teacher's guides which go beyond "here's how." Each guide on each level has been carefully planned to equip the teacher to creatively teach the unit. Spiritual challenges, unit overview, visual reinforcements, extra ideas, tips on opening and closing lessons, and special project suggestions are included in each custom-designed guide.

QUESTIONS YOU MAY HAVE

1. What is the best way to fit the character curriculum into my lesson plans?

One way is to preview each unit at the beginning of every month. Look through the teacher's guide, noting options and special events you would like to incorporate into your schedule. At the same time, decide where each worksheet best fits into your general curriculum. Then, as you write your lesson plans, include the choices from CSC.

2. Shall I set aside a time just for character study?

Yes. The amount of time set aside, however, will depend on your own schedule and goals. Some teachers reserve a small amount of daily time, while others plan a longer period once or twice a week.

3. Can one level or book be taught to children of varying ages?

Yes. This is a particularly helpful feature for teachers of split classes and for those involved in home schools. The books have been carefully designed to accommodate slow, average, and advanced students. This is done by varying the methods of completing a task (for example, drawing a line from a word to a box rather than writing it) and through use of the option and spin-off ideas accompanying most pages. It is also for this reason that clear grade level markings are absent from the covers of books.

4. Which translation of the Bible is used?

The New International Version of the Bible is used in the CSC because of its readability and broad acceptance as an excellent translation.

5. *Why is only one Bible character featured in grades two through eight?*

Viewing one Bible person from many angles of character gives the student an opportunity to become thoroughly acquainted with the strengths and weaknesses of that person. In addition, it is to the advantage of the teacher to know about whom he/she will be teaching on a continuing basis so that added materials and insights can be collected throughout the year. We believe this unique approach will have a positive effect on students and teachers.

6. *Must the verses be memorized?*

It is not necessary to lead a strenuous memorization program. However, we do encourage you to spend quality time studying and discussing God's Word. Extra credit or privileges could be awarded for memorization if you wish. Also, the theme passage for each level will be easily memorized in small pieces throughout the year.

7. *Is there music available with the curriculum?*

Yes. A songbook and cassette of a year's worth of songs are available through our office.

8. *Is there help available if I need it?*

Yes! Call us at the toll-free number listed below and we will be happy to help you.

For further information or help, please contact us at:

ACSI Headquarters
731 North Beach Blvd.
La Habra, California 90631

Mailing Address:
P.O. Box 4097
Whittier, California 90607

Toll-free phone: 1-800-423-4655

SCOPE AND SEQUENCE

The chart on the following pages outlines the traits and verses included in the study of character on each grade level.

Things to note from the Scope and Sequence chart:

1. Grades 1-8 study the same core traits at the same time. This unifies a school in its character development efforts and provides chapel leaders with an additional subject to feature during chapel time.

2. Although the traits are the same, each level has its own verse to illustrate each concept.

3. Kindergarten students study only one trait per month. That trait is either the same as one of the core traits or is similar in nature. First graders study two traits per month.

4. The title of each book is reflective of its general thrust. In the case of the second and third grade books, the title is carried out in the form of "Thought Spots" and "Life Builders." These are not additional traits but rather a practical application and/or review of the core traits.

5. Grades four through six study core traits plus one additional trait. Each additional trait is featured only once in the entire curriculum.

6. Grades seven and eight return to two core traits per unit. However, a mini-glance of a portion of the theme Scripture passage is presented in place of a third character quality. These mini-glances are called "Plus Be's."

7. Knowing the last month of school can be a special challenge for students and teachers, unit nine of each level offers an innovative review experience. More than a review of facts, this unit ties things together and gives opportunities for important reflective and practical exercises. Appropriately, the title of each book is also the title of the final unit.

8. Teachers are encouraged to insert "short-shot" verse reviews by utilizing the lists of verses on this chart. For example, a third grade teacher during unit four may choose to open class on a given morning by asking students to fill in the missing words from verses they learned about "meekness" in first and second grade.

Christian School Curriculum
SCOPE AND SEQUENCE

Level	Kindergarten	1	2	3	4	5	6	7	8
Title of Book	GETTING STARTED	DOING WHAT'S RIGHT	LEARNING TO THINK	BUILDING A LIFE	WILLING TO WAIT	PLEASING THE LORD	LIVING TO SERVE	SETTING THE GOAL	GROWING IN GRACE
Bible Character	Selected	Selected	Moses	Daniel	Nehemiah	Joshua	Esther	Joseph	David
Scripture Theme		2 Thess 3:13	Philippians 4:8,9	Psalm 34:11-13	Psalm 37:4-7, 23-24, 27-28	Psalm 25:1-5	Romans 12:13-16	Proverbs 4:13-27	Colossians 3:1-17
UNIT ONE CORE TRAIT 1	OBEDIENCE Joshua 24:24	WISDOM Proverbs 2:6	WISDOM Proverbs 8:11	WISDOM Proverbs 4:7	WISDOM Proverbs 13:20	WISDOM Proverbs 1:7	WISDOM Proverbs 19:20	WISDOM Proverbs 9:12	WISDOM Proverbs 13:10
CORE TRAIT 2		OBEDIENCE Colossians 3:20	OBEDIENCE Proverbs 10:8	OBEDIENCE Mark 4:39	OBEDIENCE Hebrews 13:17	OBEDIENCE Proverbs 13:13	OBEDIENCE Proverbs 15:12	OBEDIENCE Proverbs 15:32	OBEDIENCE Proverbs 16:20
ADDITIONAL EMPHASIS			THOUGHT SPOT	LIFE BUILDER	RESPONSIBILITY James 1:22	DISCERNMENT Proverbs 18:17	PUNCTUALITY Proverbs 10:26	PLUS BE A LEARNER Proverbs 4:13	PLUS BE HIGH MINDED Colossians 3:1-4
UNIT TWO CORE TRAIT 1	FAITH Philippians 4:13	ATTENTIVENESS Psalm 139:2	ATTENTIVENESS Proverbs 15:3	ATTENTIVENESS Psalm 118:7	ATTENTIVENESS Proverbs 4:20	ATTENTIVENESS Psalm 119:16	ATTENTIVENESS Luke 6:41,42	ATTENTIVENESS Psalm 130:2	ATTENTIVENESS Psalm 141:8
CORE TRAIT 2		FAITH 1 Corinthians 1:9	FAITH Acts 16:31	FAITH Luke 18:27	FAITH Hebrews 11:1,2	FAITH Hebrews 11:30	FAITH Hebrews 11:32-34	FAITH Hebrews 11:3	FAITH 2 Timothy 4:7
ADDITIONAL EMPHASIS			THOUGHT SPOT	LIFE BUILDER	SENSITIVITY Proverbs 25:20	CONTENTMENT Proverbs 23:4	CONFIDENCE Hebrews 13:6-8	PLUS BE A THINKER Proverbs 4:14,17	PLUS BE CLEAN HEARTED Colossians 3:5,8
UNIT THREE CORE TRAIT 1	THANKFULNESS Psalm 118:28	THANKFULNESS I Thessalonians 5:18	THANKFULNESS Psalm 75:1	THANKFULNESS Daniel 2:23	THANKFULNESS Psalm 136:1-4,26	THANKFULNESS Mark 8:6	THANKFULNESS Psalm 95:1-3	THANKFULNESS Colossians 1:3,4	THANKFULNESS Psalm 105:1,2
CORE TRAIT 2		ORDERLINESS 1 Corinthians 14:40	ORDERLINESS Proverbs 8:27	ORDERLINESS Proverbs 8:28,29	ORDERLINESS Job 38:4-7	ORDERLINESS Job 38:22-30	ORDERLINESS Esther 4:15-17	ORDERLINESS Genesis 41:33-36, 39-40	ORDERLINESS Ecclesiastes 3:1
ADDITIONAL EMPHASIS			THOUGHT SPOT	LIFE BUILDER	COURAGE Daniel 3:16-18	KINDNESS Proverbs 14:21	SINCERITY Proverbs 25:14	PLUS BE A SHINER Proverbs 4:18,19	PLUS BE CHANGING Colossians 3:9,10
UNIT FOUR CORE TRAIT 1	LOVE 1 Corinthians 16:14	MEEKNESS Proverbs 29:23	MEEKNESS Romans 12:10	MEEKNESS Psalm 25:8,9	MEEKNESS Proverbs 16:18	MEEKNESS Proverbs 25:27	MEEKNESS Romans 12:16	MEEKNESS Proverbs 25:6,7	MEEKNESS Psalm 113:5-9
CORE TRAIT 2		LOYALTY Proverbs 17:17	LOYALTY Hebrews 13:5	LOYALTY Daniel 3:16-18	LOYALTY Nehemiah 2:4,5	LOYALTY Psalm 37:28	LOYALTY Esther 8:6	LOYALTY Genesis 41:15,16	LOYALTY 2 Samuel 22:22
ADDITIONAL EMPHASIS			THOUGHT SPOT	LIFE BUILDER	JOY Nehemiah 8:10	THRIFTINESS Proverbs 17:16	REVERENCE Revelation 7:11,12	PLUS BE A LISTENER Proverbs 4:20-22	PLUS BE UNBIASED Colossians 3:11

Unit / Trait									
UNIT FIVE CORE TRAIT 1		SELF-CONTROL Proverbs 29:11	SELF-CONTROL Proverbs 21:23	SELF-CONTROL Proverbs 14:17	SELF-CONTROL Proverbs 22:24	SELF-CONTROL Proverbs 25:28	SELF-CONTROL Proverbs 17:27	SELF-CONTROL Proverbs 16:28	SELF-CONTROL 1 Peter 5:8
CORE TRAIT 2	HONESTY Proverbs 12:22	HONESTY Ephesians 4:25	HONESTY Leviticus 19:11	HONESTY Proverbs 12:22	HONESTY Proverbs 17:20	HONESTY Proverbs 17:20	HONESTY Proverbs 16:13	HONESTY Proverbs 17:7	HONESTY Proverbs 15:4
ADDITIONAL EMPHASIS			THOUGHT SPOT	LIFE BUILDER	HELPFULNESS Psalm 121:1-4	DECISIVENESS 1 Kings 3:5,9	CAUTIOUSNESS Proverbs 12:26	PLUS BE A PROTECTOR Proverbs 4:23	PLUS BE UNDERSTANDING Colossians 3:12-14
UNIT SIX CORE TRAIT 1		DILIGENCE Colossians 3:23	DILIGENCE Proverbs 10:4	DILIGENCE Daniel 6:10	DILIGENCE Nehemiah 6:15	DILIGENCE Joshua 22:1-4	DILIGENCE Proverbs 25:13	DILIGENCE Proverbs 21:5	DILIGENCE John 17:4
CORE TRAIT 2	PERSEVERANCE Ecclesiastes 9:10	PATIENCE 1 Corinthians 13:4	PATIENCE Proverbs 19:11	PATIENCE Psalm 103:8	PATIENCE Proverbs 15:18	PATIENCE Psalm 37:7	PATIENCE James 5:7,8	PATIENCE Proverbs 16:32	PATIENCE Psalm 27:14
ADDITIONAL EMPHASIS			THOUGHT SPOT	LIFE BUILDER	DEPENDABILITY 2 Chronicles 31:21	ENDURANCE Psalm 125:1	THOROUGHNESS Psalm 138:8	PLUS BE A TRUE TALKER Proverbs 4:24	PLUS BE PEACE LOVING Colossians 3:15
UNIT SEVEN CORE TRAIT 1		FORGIVENESS Colossians 3:13b	FORGIVENESS Matthew 5:44	FORGIVENESS Psalm 86:5	FORGIVENESS Proverbs 14:9	FORGIVENESS Psalm 32:1,2	FORGIVENESS Proverbs 20:22	FORGIVENESS Genesis 50:19-21	FORGIVENESS Psalm 51:1-4
CORE TRAIT 2	FRIENDLINESS Proverbs 17:17	FAIRNESS Romans 13:9	FAIRNESS 1 Tim 5:21	FAIRNESS Matthew 7:12	FAIRNESS James 2:1-4	FAIRNESS Romans 15:7	FAIRNESS Proverbs 18:5	FAIRNESS Psalm 112:5	FAIRNESS Isaiah 5:22,23
ADDITIONAL EMPHASIS			THOUGHT SPOT	LIFE BUILDER	TOLERANCE Psalm 133:1	GENEROSITY Proverbs 28:27	FRIENDLINESS Proverbs 27:9	PLUS BE A WATCHER Proverbs 4:25	PLUS BE OUTSPOKEN Colossians 3:16
UNIT EIGHT CORE TRAIT 1		INITIATIVE Philippians 2:4	INITIATIVE Isaiah 6:8	INITIATIVE Daniel 2:14-16	INITIATIVE Nehemiah 2:4,5	INITIATIVE Proverbs 6:6-8	INITIATIVE James 1:22	INITIATIVE Proverbs 22:29	INITIATIVE Ephesians 5:15,16
CORE TRAIT 2	KINDNESS Isaiah 41:6	LOVE John 15:12b	LOVE John 14:15	LOVE John 15:9	LOVE Romans 13:10	LOVE Psalm 62:11,12	LOVE 1 Peter 4:8	LOVE Hebrews 13:1,2	LOVE Romans 12:9
ADDITIONAL EMPHASIS			THOUGHT SPOT	LIFE BUILDER	RESOURCEFULNESS Proverbs 16:3	CREATIVITY Genesis 2:4-7	BOLDNESS Psalm 138:3	PLUS BE A WALKER Proverbs 4:26,27	PLUS BE WHOLEHEARTED Colossians 3:17
UNIT NINE REVIEW	GETTING STARTED	DOING WHAT'S RIGHT	LEARNING TO THINK	BUILDING A LIFE	WILLING TO WAIT	PLEASING THE LORD	LIVING TO SERVE	SETTING THE GOAL	GROWING IN GRACE

INTRODUCTION
to
LIVING TO SERVE

You have the happy privilege of counteracting a myth that has tried to sweep away the foundation of true happiness. The myth? Think of yourself first. The foundation that has been eroded? Think of others first. Of course, the myth is nothing new. It is simply selfishness in make-up and modernized. But, then, the foundation is nothing new either. It is as old as God Himself – and as young.

The focus of this book is the same as its title: Living To Serve. It has been carefully designed to help you help your students explore the joys and benefits of serving God and others.

As an encouragement in learning to serve, and as a tool for character training, the student book and teacher's guide for LIVING TO SERVE include the following features:

Student Book

The student book includes:

TRAITS, DEFINITIONS, OPPOSITES, AND TRAIT VERSES that explain each concept. Three traits are presented in units one through eight. The Mini-Unit introduces the book to the student, and Unit Nine reviews all traits. Each unit is designed to last approximately one month.

UNIT INTRODUCTION DESIGNER PAGES that stimulate thought and creativity. They include the unit's theme verse and main thrust.

ACTIVITY SHEETS that lead the student in exploring the meaning of each character trait.

SERVANT PROJECT STORIES that bring the character qualities to life in today's world.

ESTHER

ESTHER STUDIES that appear once per unit and include an illustration, a story, and a comprehension check-up.

ILLUSTRATIONS AND DESIGN that are beautifully blended to appeal to students at this level.

Teacher's Guide

The teacher's guide includes:

STEP ONE devotionals that challenge and initiate personal application of the traits being studied in each unit.

SPECIFICS pages that provide the teacher with a quick reference of unit content, as well as enrichment suggestions.

SPIN-OFF suggestions that are scattered throughout the text of instructions. These are in addition to the ideas and visual reinforcements found on the Specifics page.

REDUCED STUDENT PAGES that include answers to student activity sheets.

ACTIVITY SHEET INSTRUCTIONS that offer you a systematic method of presenting each page of the student book.

FOLLOW-UP QUESTIONS that measure student understanding of the servant stories and provide you with help in stimulating the imaginations of your students.

BACKFIRE! A MELODRAMA that provides you with a ready-made performance and reinforcement tool. Included are set design and costume tips, script, and program cover design.

PROJECT SERVANT

PROJECT SERVANT ideas that help you lead your students into actual acts of service.

HELPING CHILDREN LEARN TO SERVE

Teaching character does not mean you must have all of the answers to life issues. In fact, it means having the character to admit that you don't! Allow your students to be children, yourself to be human, and your God to be God.

The theme of this book, LIVING TO SERVE, sets the stage for you to lead a sixth grade team of explorers through the ins and outs of servanthood. As their leader, you will be watched closely by those who follow. They will want to see you serve first so that they will know what service looks like. In order to model servanthood confidently, we suggest that you analyze your own perception of servanthood. Define it, update it, and ask God to renew your belief in it.

Be aware that all of your students may not have trusted Jesus Christ as their Savior. Often children in Christian schools are embarrassed to admit that they have not yet made that commitment. Let your students know that you are aware that they may not yet be believers, and assure them of your interest at any time in helping them come to a decision.

DISCUSSION SUGGESTIONS

1. Encourage imaginative thought by taking a question beyond its initial stage. Example: Now that you have correctly defined "even-tempered," please suppose that you were in the company of an even-tempered woman when she was told her children had spilled cranberry juice on the rug. What might she say?

2. Praise good ideas, insight, and logic. Monitor yourself to insure that verbal pleasure over student performance remains a priority.

3. Carry discussions through these levels of thought:

LEVEL ONE: FACTS – Who did what, when?
LEVEL TWO: METHOD – How was it done?
LEVEL THREE: REASON – Why was it done?
LEVEL FOUR: THOUGHT – What idea was behind it?
LEVEL FIVE: CHOICE – What will I do or think?

SCHEDULING TIPS

The scheduling of this curriculum is to be determined by you, the teacher. We suggest that you read through each unit, select any optional activities you wish to use, then place each activity into your overall lesson plan where it fits the best. Note your choices in "My Plan for the Unit," then evaluate their success in "Next-Time Notes." Many of the activities in LIVING TO SERVE are suitable for use during language arts and Bible, while others would fit well in science, math, or music.

MUSIC

A songbook and cassette tape called "Growing Up God's Way" contain thirty-one character building songs to enhance this curriculum. An added feature is the ability of the cassette to become an instrumental background tape for performance with the turn of the balance knob on any stereo. The set may be ordered by calling ACSI headquarters at 1-800-423-4655.

Just as the key to happiness is serving others, the key to understanding this book is teaching it. We wish you well on your journey through LIVING TO SERVE!

VERSE AND TRAIT LIST FOR LIVING TO SERVE

THEME VERSE FOR THE YEAR:
Romans 12:13-16
"Share with God's people who are in need. Practice hospitality. Bless those who persecute you; bless and do not curse. Rejoice with those who rejoice; mourn with those who mourn. Live in harmony with one another. Do not be proud, but be willing to associate with people of low position. Do not be conceited."

WISDOM: Proverbs 19:20
"Listen to advice and accept instruction, and in the end you will be wise."
> **DEFINITION:** Using what I know of God to make sound decisions.
> **OPPOSITE:** Leaving God out of my decisions.

OBEDIENCE: Proverbs 15:12
"A mocker resents correction; he will not consult the wise."
> **DEFINITION:** Doing what I am told to do.
> **OPPOSITE:** Doing what I am told not to do.

PUNCTUALITY: Proverbs 10:26
"As vinegar to the teeth and smoke to the eyes, so is a sluggard to those who send him."
> **DEFINITION:** Being on time.
> **OPPOSITE:** Being late.

ATTENTIVENESS: Luke 6:41, 42
"Why do you look at the speck of sawdust in your brother's eye and pay no attention to the plank in your own eye? How can you say to your brother, 'Brother, let me take the speck out of your eye,' when you yourself fail to see the plank in your own eye? You hypocrite, first take the plank out of your eye, and then you will see clearly to remove the speck from your brother's eye."
> **DEFINITION:** Watching and listening closely to what is happening.
> **OPPOSITE:** Neglecting to notice what is happening.

FAITH: Hebrews 11:32-34
"And what more shall I say? I do not have time to tell about Gideon, Barak, Samson, Jephthah, David, Samuel and the prophets, who through faith conquered kingdoms, administered justice, and gained what was promised; who shut the mouths of lions, quenched the fury of the flames, and escaped the edge of the sword; whose weakness was turned to strength; and who became powerful in battle and routed foreign armies."
> **DEFINITION:** Believing God will do what He says He will do.
> **OPPOSITE:** Disbelieving God.

CONFIDENCE: Hebrews 13:6-8
"So we say with confidence, 'The Lord is my helper; I will not be afraid. What can man do to me?' Remember your leaders, who spoke the word of God to you. Consider the outcome of their way of life and imitate their faith. Jesus Christ is the same yesterday and today and forever."
> **DEFINITION:** A strong belief in the ability of a person or thing.
> **OPPOSITE:** Doubting the abilities of a person or thing.

THANKFULNESS: Psalm 95:1-3
"Come, let us sing for joy to the Lord; let us shout aloud to the Rock of our salvation. Let us come before Him with thanksgiving and extol Him with music and song. For the Lord is the great God, the great King above all gods."
> **DEFINITION:** Being glad for the goodness of God and others.
> **OPPOSITE:** Being blind to the goodness of God and others.

ORDERLINESS: Esther 4:15-17
"Then Esther sent this reply to Mordecai: 'Go, gather together all the Jews who are in Susa, and fast for me. Do not eat or drink for three days, night or day. I and my maids will fast as you do. When this is done, I will go to the king, even though it is against the law. And if I perish, I perish.' "
> **DEFINITION:** Putting things and plans in their right place.
> **OPPOSITE:** Allowing things and plans to become confusing.

SINCERITY: Proverbs 25:14
"Like clouds and wind without rain is a man who boasts of gifts he does not give."
> **DEFINITION:** Truly meaning what I say and do.
> **OPPOSITE:** Pretending that I mean what I say and do.

MEEKNESS: Romans 12:16
"Live in harmony with one another. Do not be proud, but be willing to associate with people of low position. Do not be conceited."
   DEFINITION: Serving others with the abilities God has given me.
   OPPOSITE: Showing off with the abilities God has given me.

LOYALTY: Esther 8:6
"For how can I bear to see disaster fall on my people? How can I bear to see the destruction of my family?"
   DEFINITION: Staying true to those I serve.
   OPPOSITE: Staying true to only myself.

REVERENCE: Revelation 7:11, 12
"All the angels were standing around the throne and around the elders and the four living creatures. They fell down on their faces before the throne and worshipped God, saying: 'Amen! Praise and glory and wisdom and thanks and honor and power and strength be to our God for ever and ever. Amen!' "
   DEFINITION: A deep respect and awe for someone.
   OPPOSITE: Not thinking very highly of someone.

SELF-CONTROL: Proverbs 17:27
"A man of knowledge uses words with restraint, and a man of understanding is even-tempered."
   DEFINITION: Guarding my life by making right choices.
   OPPOSITE: Letting anything into my life.

HONESTY: Proverbs 16:13
"Kings take pleasure in honest lips; they value a man who speaks the truth."
   DEFINITION: Being free of lies.
   OPPOSITE: Being full of lies.

CAUTIOUSNESS: Proverbs 12:26
"A righteous man is cautious in friendship, but the way of the wicked leads them astray."
   DEFINITION: Living my life carefully.
   OPPOSITE: Not caring how I live my life.

DILIGENCE: Proverbs 25:13
"Like the coolness of snow at harvest time is a trustworthy messenger to those who send him; he refreshes the spirit of his masters."
   DEFINITION: Doing my work steadily until it is done.
   OPPOSITE: Quitting when I feel like it.

PATIENCE: James 5:7, 8
"Be patient, then, brothers, until the Lord's coming. See how the farmer waits for the land to yield its valuable crop and how patient he is for the autumn and spring rains. You too, be patient and stand firm, because the Lord's coming is near."
   DEFINITION: Choosing to wait with calmness.
   OPPOSITE: Letting anger rule my waiting.

THOROUGHNESS: Psalm 138:8
"The Lord will fulfill His purpose for me; Your love, O Lord, endures forever – do not abandon the works of Your hands."
   DEFINITION: Completing the details of a task.
   OPPOSITE: Overlooking the details of a task.

FORGIVENESS: Proverbs 20:22
"Do not say, 'I'll pay you back for this wrong!' Wait for the Lord, and He will deliver you."
   DEFINITION: Caring more about God than my grudge.
   OPPOSITE: Caring more about my grudge than about God.

FAIRNESS: Proverbs 18:5
"It is not good to be partial to the wicked or to deprive the innocent of justice."
   DEFINITION: Judging a situation correctly.
   OPPOSITE: Showing favorites in my decisions.

FRIENDLINESS: Proverbs 27:9
"Perfume and incense bring joy to the heart, and the pleasantness of one's friend springs from his earnest counsel."
   DEFINITION: Reaching out to others in a warm-hearted way.
   OPPOSITE: Responding with coolness to those around me.

INITIATIVE: James 1:22
"Do not merely listen to the word, and so deceive yourselves. Do what it says."
   DEFINITION: Carrying an idea from my mind into reality.
   OPPOSITE: Letting others get things started.

LOVE: I Peter 4:8
"Above all, love each other deeply, because love covers over a multitude of sins."
   DEFINITION: Caring strongly for a person or thing.
   OPPOSITE: Not caring about a person or thing.

BOLDNESS: Psalm 138:3
"When I called, You answered me; You made me bold and stouthearted."
   DEFINITION: Facing life in a daring way.
   OPPOSITE: Facing life in a cowardly way.

STEP ONE

Beginnings. Behind those sets of eyes looking at us are minds compiling data and projecting the success of the year with us as their teachers. They are preparing to answer the traditional first-day-of-the-year question: "What is your teacher like?" But the question they are asking themselves is: "Will this teacher love me?" As teachers "standing in" for God, the only answer is "Yes, we will love you!"

Yes. We will love you. We will show God's character by how we teach and talk and act. We will reach out to you no matter how you dress or smell or speak, because we do not have the freedom to be choosey. We have been called to care unconditionally.

Yes. We will love you. We will create an environment of safety and a refuge from insults and abuse. A place where a wrong answer goes without ridicule and where mistakes are kept in perspective.

Yes. We will love you. We will study and creatively teach in a way we would enjoy if we were in our class. We will establish a few solid rules of behavior and enforce them fairly in a controlled manner, apart from the rest of the class.

Yes. We will love you. We will introduce you to the God we love, the God who is right now reading your minds and preparing to meet your needs through us.

PATTERNING

Often God's first words to His children have been, "Fear not." He set them at ease, or at least let them know He was visiting in peace. Following His example, make a planned effort to call a few parents each day this month to say a peaceful word about their child. Let them know you are glad to be their child's teacher and invite them to call you at any time with questions or concerns. This act of kindness will not be forgotten.

CHEWABLES
Bite-sized thoughts from God's Word

"Show me Your ways, O Lord, teach me Your paths; guide me in Your truth and teach me, for you are God my Savior, and my hope is in You all day long." Psalm 25:4, 5

"The LORD will fulfill his purpose for me; Your love, O LORD, endures forever – do not abandon the works of Your hands." Psalm 138:8

"Love never fails." I Corinthians 13:8

Because this is an introductory unit, the usual features of all other units are not applicable.

UNIT INFORMATION

Purpose:
To introduce the students to this book, to the concept of serving others, to the Esther study, and to the servant stories.

Approach:
Welcome to the book.

Definition:
N/A

Opposite:
N/A

Trait Verse:
N/A

Visual Reinforcement:
Cut out and glitter the letters in LIVING TO ??? Place on a bulletin board. Invite students to draw or cut out pictures of various things people live for.

Ideas:
After reading the unit servant story, instruct students to write brief personality summaries of the main characters in the story. Staple them to the inside cover of the book so that the student can compare their initial impressions with the final outcome.

Use as Desired:
N/A

MY PLAN FOR THIS UNIT

_____

_____

_____

_____

3 LIVING TO SERVE

- Read through the text with your students.
  - ◗ Stop to question and briefly discuss each section.
- The First Step
  - ◗ Allow time for students to formulate opinions about each statement.
  - ◗ Call on students to offer their opinions.

NOTE: This exercise will set the stage for future discussions. Make certain that you provide room for differences of opinion, and avoid a lecture-type atmosphere to spoil authentic interaction. If students tend to give "pat" answers to the questions, re-phrase them, then follow up with extended questions that force students to think and respond honestly. Thinkers should feel at home in the Christian classroom.

◗ Ask students to name the main sources of these statements of thought.

4 ESTHER ILLUSTRATION

- Study and discuss the pictures of the cast of characters.

Living To Serve

THE IDEA

Here is an idea that may sound odd to you: Serve others and you will find the secret of happiness. The reason it may sound odd is that it has been changed around to sound like this: Serve yourself and you will find the secret of happiness.

The first idea is the one that came from the mind of God. The second idea came from the mind of people. It is up to you to choose whose mind to trust.

THE BOOK

This book takes God's idea of serving others and explores it. It helps you see how serving others is done and gives you ways to try it yourself.

In the book, you will meet a woman who served her country, some kids who serve all kinds of people, and the true God who serves the universe.

THE PLAN

By looking at the Table of Contents you can see how the book is organized. By looking at the titles of the units, you can see the ways of serving that you will be studying. The servant stories were planned for you by students your age. They had fun swapping good ideas and thinking of you.

Some people live to eat. Others live to play sports. Still others live to be with their friends. There are other people who like to eat, play sports, *and* be with their friends. But more than anything they like to serve. It is what they live for. These people are the ones who have found the key to happiness.

We could say that the main plan of this book is to help you understand one of God's main plans: Living To Serve.

THE FIRST STEP

Read these popular statements about being a servant. Do you agree or disagree with them? Be prepared to express your opinion about each one to the class.

Statement #1: Caring about others more than yourself is old-fashioned.

Statement #2: If you don't look out for Number One, who will?

Statement #3: If you serve people, they will expect you to be their slave.

Statement #4: If I serve others all of the time, there won't be any time left for myself!

Esther, Mordecai, King Xerxes, Haman and Vashti in one of history's most daring dramas.

5 BACKFIRE: Introduction To The Esther Story

NOTE: The BACKFIRE stories tell about Queen Esther's courageous actions on behalf of her people. The suspense builds with each episode and finally reaches a climax in Unit Seven. Encourage students who are familiar with the story to keep from going into great detail about it. Remember, a melodrama of the story is located in the back of this book.

- Ask students to define the various meanings of backfire.
  ◆ In this case, it represents the turnaround of Haman's wicked scheme to kill all of the Jews in Persia.
- Read each synopsis. Discuss as desired.

ESTHER

This book features the exciting Bible story of Esther. It happened about 500 years before Jesus was born, and takes place in the kingdom of Persia at a time when the Jews were living away from Canaan.

The people you will meet in the story are:

Esther

Esther had grown to be a beautiful young woman. Her parents had died when she was a child, so her cousin, Mordecai, adopted her. As a child playing near the palace, Esther might have dreamed of being the queen, but she could never have guessed that a nation of people would rely on her to save them from an evil massacre.

Mordecai

An officer in the king's household, Mordecai was a faithful Jew and a loyal servant of King Xerxes. He proved his loyalty to the king by uncovering a plot to assassinate him. This brave action later led the king to reward Mordecai in a way that made Haman sorry he ever opened his mouth.

King Xerxes

After King Darius died, Asahuerus, or Xerxes, became king of Persia. King Xerxes seemed to enjoy being a king, and he especially relished the feasts and parties. He was proud of his kingdom and liked showing it off. King Xerxes seemed to trust almost anyone in his palace, which nearly cost him his life and the life of his queen.

Queen Vashti

King Xerxes' pride over his kingdom included his beautiful wife, Vashti. She was not only beautiful, but was stubborn in her ideas about herself. This would one day turn the kingdom – and her crown – upside down.

Haman

Haman loved collecting power for himself. Pride oozed from his words and splashed across his conceited smile. He was able to lie in ways that caused the king and others to believe him. Haman's wickedness kept the Jews hanging in fear, but a sudden turn of events kept Haman hanging forever.

6 SERVANT STORY: THE HENRY PROJECT

- Read the story.
  ◆ Discuss the events, recalling facts and using "What if" questions to stimulate thought about other ways the story could have ended.

SERVANT STORY

The Henry Project

Tony ran screaming into his house. "Miss Pam! Miss Pam! Call the ambulance. A kid's been hit by a car!"

Miss Pam hurried to the phone, dropping a pile of laundry on the way. Tony ran back outside to join the crowd that had gathered around the boy.

Tony's heart skipped a beat when he realized that the boy was Henry Klinkdale. Henry and Tony, or "Bounce," as his teammates called him, played basketball on the same Boys' Club team. "Henry, it's me, Tony Erving. You know, 'Bounce' . . . from the team." Henry looked toward the familiar voice. "An ambulance is on its way. You're going to be fine. Really!"

"Jerome. Where's Jerome?" whispered Henry.

Tony didn't need to look far to see the scraggly tail of the mutt Henry called Jerome. He was being held back by a well-meaning observer and was only about two feet from Henry's head. "He's right over there," said Tony. "I'll see you at the hospital," yelled Tony as they closed the doors of the van.

Tony's thoughts carried him back three years to the accident that had killed his mother. She had been on her way to buy decorations for his eighth birthday party. Seeing Henry hurt caused Tony to feel ill.

"Tony! Is he going to be all right?" called Miss Pam from the porch. Miss Pam was the Erving's housekeeper. "Yes," hollered Tony. "It looks like

a broken leg. He's a kid who plays on my Boys' Club team and I promised him I would take his dog home. I'll be right back. Okay?"

As Tony and Jerome rounded the corner, Betty Canterbury caught up with them. "I heard about Henry! His dad is our gardener." The closer they got to Henry's house, the poorer looking the houses became. Henry's home was too small for the six children and two parents who lived there, but it was neatly kept. "I like the color they have painted their house," said Betty.

Betty's own house was at least ten times larger than the Klinkdale's home, but she was not one to be snobbish about her wealth. The family was hurrying to their beat up station wagon to go to the hospital, but they stopped long enough to give Tony a sincere thanks for returning Jerome.

The next day at the lunch table, Tony and Betty continued talking about Henry. Their visit to Henry's house had caused them to want to do something to help. "My dad said that Henry has an afternoon paper route that helps pay for his brother's diabetes medicine," said Betty.

Soon David Peterson and Darcie Carlisle had joined them. Darcie didn't know Henry, but David did. He had tutored Henry in reading last quarter. The four began pooling ideas about ways to help Henry. They gradually agreed to a plan of action. David scribbled their ideas onto Tony's lunch sack, then later he transferred them to his computer. The following day, he gave each member of the group a print-out of The Henry Project.

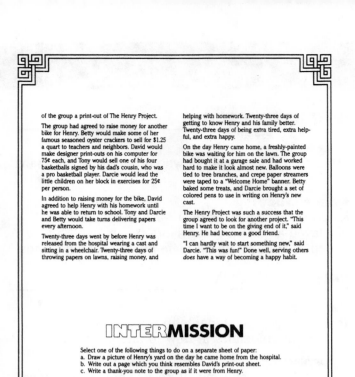

of the group a print-out of The Henry Project.

The group had agreed to raise money for another bike for Henry. Betty would make some of her famous seasoned oyster crackers to sell for $1.25 a quart to teachers and neighbors. David would make designer print-outs on his computer for 75¢ each, and Tony would sell one of his four basketballs signed by his dad's cousin, who was a pro basketball player. Darcie would lead the little children on her block in exercises for 25¢ per person.

In addition to raising money for the bike, David agreed to help Henry with his homework until he was able to return to school. Tony and Darcie and Betty would take turns delivering papers every afternoon.

Twenty-three days went by before Henry was released from the hospital wearing a cast and sitting in a wheelchair. Twenty-three days of throwing papers on lawns, raising money, and helping with homework. Twenty-three days of getting to know Henry and his family better. Twenty-three days of being extra tired, extra helpful, and extra happy.

On the day Henry came home, a freshly-painted bike was waiting for him on the lawn. The group had bought it at a garage sale and had worked hard to make it look almost new. Balloons were tied to tree branches, and crepe paper streamers were taped to a "Welcome Home" banner. Betty baked some treats, and Darcie brought a set of colored pens to use in writing on Henry's new cast.

The Henry Project was such a success that the group agreed to look for another project. "This time I want to be on the giving end of it," said Henry. He had become a good friend.

"I can hardly wait to start something new," said Darcie. "This was fun!" Done well, serving others *does* have a way of becoming a happy habit.

INTERMISSION

Select one of the following things to do on a separate sheet of paper:
a. Draw a picture of Henry's yard on the day he came home from the hospital.
b. Write out a page which you think resembles David's print-out sheet.
c. Write a thank-you note to the group as if it were from Henry.

- Intermission
  - Instruct students to complete one of the suggested activities.
  - Collect, comment, and display as desired.

A child's life is like a piece of paper
upon which every passerby leaves
a mark.

Ancient Chinese Proverb

STEP ONE

Wisdom may not carry chalk, but she is a teacher all right. She raises her voice, climbs walls, gives talks, and wonders if anyone is listening (Pr. 1:20-23). She is a principal's fantasy: intense yet gentle, practical yet creative, and always ready to help.

We who do carry chalk would be smart to ask for her help. This month she could teach us something about herself, as well as obedience and punctuality.

Of particular interest is the role of wisdom in giving and receiving commands. God says, "The wise in heart accepts commands" (Pr. 10:8). Our students will be wise to obey our commands. At the same time, we will be wise to give them in a way that accurately reflects the teaching methods of God.

Generally, when God gives a command, He states it clearly. When He teaches, His lessons are creative, challenging, and personalized. He is fair, and His reinforcements are ample. His goals are realistic, and His love is unconditional. These ingredients belong in our teaching treasury as well.

Obeying the commands of God is the responsibility of we who have put ourselves under His leadership. Follow the Leader is more than child's play; it is the stuff from which great teachers are made.

PATTERNING

How wise are your classroom commands? Take a sheet of paper and write these titles across the top of the page, forming five columns: Commands, How told, Consequences, Wise?, Adjustments. List the commands, or rules, of your room, how you communicate them, and the consequences of disobedience. Evaluate your chart through the filter of wisdom and make necessary adjustments.

CHEWABLES
Bite-sized thoughts from God's Word

Select a thought to "chew on" during this unit:

"I run in the path of Your commands, for You have set my heart free."   Psalm 119:32

"All Your commands are trustworthy."   Psalm 119:86

"This has been my practice: I obey Your precepts."
                                             Psalm 119:56

UNIT INFORMATION

Theme Verse:
"Share with God's people who are in need." Romans 12:13

Esther Study:
King Xerxes is furious over Vashti's refusal to be displayed at his party. Advisors recommend a new queen. He agrees to the plan. Beauty search begins.

PART A: WISDOM

Purpose:
To encourage the students to seek advice.
To present guidelines in how to find good advice.

Approach:
The most successful and interesting people are those who never stop learning.
Asking for advice shows that I am being wise.

Definition:
Using what I know of God to make sound decisions.

Opposite:
Leaving God out of my decisions.

Trait Verse:
Proverbs 19:20
"Listen to advice and accept instruction, and in the end you will be wise."

Visual Reinforcement:
Have some students volunteer to create an attractive poster displaying the unit's subtitle (Serving by Sharing) and theme verse. Display this poster conspicuously during the unit.

Make a bulletin board using the Bible verse. Title it "Some Good Advice: Take Advice!" Write out the verse under the title. Fill the board with common questions facing your students, and scatter brightly colored question marks over it.

Ideas:
Collect copies of advice columns. Select some letters, without including the answers, to distribute to your students. Ask them to give advice to the writer. Compare the advice. If desired, read the actual advice given.

Use as Desired:
SP 9, Good Advice, Bad Advice
SP 10, Dear David
TG 88, Project Servant

PART B: OBEDIENCE

Purpose:
To demonstrate how one loses by disobedience, and how one gains by obedience.
To spotlight the main issue as one of selfishness.

Approach:
Everyone needs to be corrected at times.
If I learn to accept correction, I will be showing wisdom.
When I'm disobeying, I am being stubbornly selfish.

Definition:
Doing what I am told to do.

Opposite:
Doing what I am told not to do.

Trait Verse:
Proverbs 15:12
"A mocker resents correction; he will not consult the wise."

Servant Story:
Tony's temper stalls the project until the group and Mr. Newman help give him perspective.

Visual Reinforcement:
Using several orange circles to represent the basketball in the Project Servant obedience story, print the trait verse and other verses from Proverbs which speak of correction or obedience. Use the circles, or basketballs, as flashcard-style discussion starters. For example, using the trait verse, ask, "What are some common corrections that sixth graders are given?"

Ideas:
Invite a counselor to speak to your class about ways to give and receive good advice. Prior to the visit, present a brief study about the role of counselors. You may also wish to divide your class into small groups, instructing each group to compose three questions for the counselor.

Use as Desired:
SP 11, Working Things Out

PART C: PUNCTUALITY

Purpose:
To study the habits of the punctual.

Approach:
Punctuality brings me many good things.
I can learn to be punctual.

Definition:
Being on time.

Opposite:
Being late.

Trait Verse:
Proverbs 10:26
"As vinegar to the teeth and smoke to the eyes, so is a sluggard to those who send him."

Visual Reinforcement:
On a bulletin board, place a replica of a large clock and the words "Punctuality Pays." Around the clock, place sentence cards written by students stating the benefits one can receive by being punctual and/or true experiences of being punctual or late.

Ideas:
Award a certificate of punctuality to those who are on time to class and in homework submission during the unit. Present the awards in chapel, if desired, adding that because of the time saved by the students being punctual, they will receive a portion of free time in class.

Conduct interviews by students of parents and friends to discover the similarities and differences in people's schedules and habits of punctuality. As a class, select questions to be asked. A team of students compile the results and report them promptly to the class.

Use as Desired:
SP 14, Punctuality Plan Activated

MY PLAN FOR THIS UNIT

_____

_____

_____

_____

A NOTE ABOUT INTRODUCING A UNIT:
The purpose behind the design of the unit introductory pages is (1) to designate the beginning of a new section, (2) to present the part of the theme verse to be studied, (3) to present the three traits that will be studied, and (4) to permit you and your students to focus on examples of serving that are found surrounding the life of Jesus.

Students will be asked to color the page attractively with marking pens. We suggest that you read the example from the Bible which is given in the teacher's guide, then discuss the issues with your students.

8 INTRO TO UNIT

- Read over information on page together.
- Briefly discuss the idea of sharing with those in need. Provide true life examples from your own life, if possible.
- Instruct students to begin inking in the design.
  ◗ As they begin, read the class the following passages aloud, briefly summarizing each one:
  2 Cor. 8:1-4
  2 Cor. 8:13-15
  2 Cor. 9:6-12
- Circulate, praising and encouraging your students.
- Conclude the session with a discussion of what is happening now in families, churches, and schools to help the needy.

9 WISDOM

- Read trait information together.
  ◗ Call on students to repeat it back to you.
  ◗ Lead class in a lively drill of Proverbs 19:20.
- Read "Lesson Learning."
  ◗ Discuss the boys' two points of view.
  ◗ Recall Bible words from the trait verse about instruction.
  ◗ Ask, "Which of the two viewpoints would God call wise?"
- Complete questions.
  ◗ Discuss answers and compare experiences.

SPIN-OFF
Good advice, Bad Advice. Post student ideas of good advice and bad advice about issues and behavior relating to sixth graders.

Serve your students by sharing and showing wisdom.

UNIT ONE
Serving by Sharing

"Share with God's people who are in need." Romans 12:13

WISDOM ♦ OBEDIENCE ♦ PUNCTUALITY

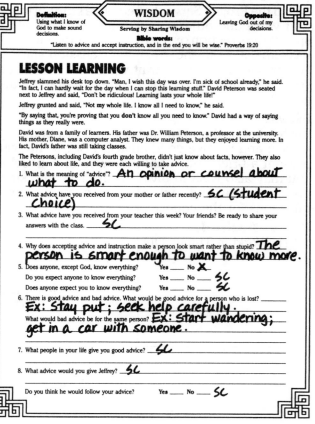

Definition: Using what I know of God to make sound decisions.

WISDOM
Serving by Sharing Wisdom

Opposite: Leaving God out of my decisions.

Bible words:
"Listen to advice and accept instruction, and in the end you will be wise." Proverbs 19:20

LESSON LEARNING

Jeffrey slammed his desk top down. "Man, I wish this day were over. I'm sick of school already," he said. "In fact, I can hardly wait for the day when I can stop this learning stuff." David Peterson was seated next to Jeffrey and said, "Don't be ridiculous! Learning lasts your whole life!"

Jeffrey grunted and said, "Not my whole life. I know all I need to know," he said.

"By saying that, you're proving that you **don't** know all you need to know." David had a way of saying things as they really were.

David was from a family of learners. His father was Dr. William Peterson, a professor at the university. His mother, Diane, was a computer analyst. They knew many things, but they enjoyed learning more. In fact, David's father was still taking classes.

The Petersons, including David's fourth grade brother, didn't just know about facts, however. They also liked to learn about life, and they were each willing to take advice.

1. What is the meaning of "advice"? An opinion or counsel about what to do.

2. What advice have you received from your mother or father recently? SC (student choice)

3. What advice have you received from your teacher this week? Your friends? Be ready to share your answers with the class. SC

4. Why does accepting advice and instruction make a person look smart rather than stupid? The person is smart enough to want to know more.

5. Does anyone, except God, know everything? Yes ___ No X
   Do you expect anyone to know everything? Yes ___ No ___ SC
   Does anyone expect you to know everything? Yes ___ No ___ SC

6. Is good advice and bad advice. What would be good advice for a person who is lost? ___ Ex: Stay put; seek help carefully.
   What would bad advice be for the same person? Ex: Start wandering; get in a car with someone.

7. What people in your life give you good advice? SC

8. What advice would you give Jeffrey? SC

   Do you think he would follow your advice? Yes ___ No ___ SC

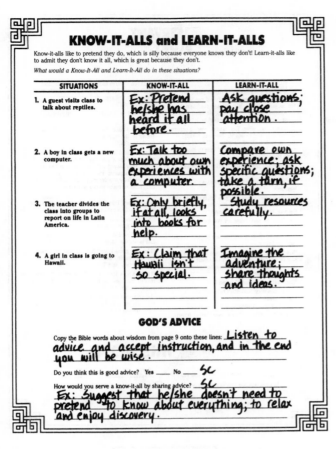

KNOW-IT-ALLS and LEARN-IT-ALLS

Know-it-alls like to pretend they do, which is silly because everyone knows they don't! Learn-it-alls like to admit they don't know it all, which is great because they don't.

What would a Know-It-All and Learn-It-All do in these situations?

SITUATIONS	KNOW-IT-ALL	LEARN-IT-ALL
1. A guest visits class to talk about reptiles.	Ex: Pretend he/she has heard it all before.	Ask questions; pay close attention.
2. A boy in class gets a new computer.	Ex: Talk too much about own experiences with a computer.	Compare own experience; ask specific questions; take a turn, if possible.
3. The teacher divides the class into groups to report on life in Latin America.	Ex: Only briefly, if at all, looks into books for help.	Study resources carefully.
4. A girl in class is going to Hawaii.	Ex: Claim that Hawaii isn't so special.	Imagine the adventure; share thoughts and ideas.

GOD'S ADVICE

Copy the Bible words about wisdom from page 9 onto these lines: Listen to advice and accept instruction, and in the end you will be wise.

Do you think this is good advice? Yes ____ No ____ SC

How would you serve a know-it-all by sharing advice? SC
Ex: Suggest that he/she doesn't need to pretend to know about everything; to relax and enjoy discovery.

Definition: Doing what I am told to do.	OBEDIENCE	Opposite: Doing what I am told not to do.
	Serving by Doing What I'm Told	

Bible words:
"A mocker resents correction; he will not consult the wise." Proverbs 15:12

SERVANT STORY

Sharing The Load

The day Henry said, "I wish we could think of a way to let the teachers know we appreciate them" was the day the group's second project began.

Because of his cast, Henry had been helping Mrs. Maddux in the art room instead of going to PE. He was amazed at how much work she had to do every day. At lunch, he would talk about it to the group.

"I hardly ever see a teacher leave the school without carrying work home," said Betty. The others agreed.

And so, when Henry spoke his wish about showing appreciation, all the members of the group were ready to do something about it. What they did was plan a Be-Good-to-Teacher Week.

As usual, David was quick to make things official with a computer print-out of their Agreement to Appreciate. It contained the plans of the Be-Good-to-Teacher project. They wanted to obey and help in such a way that teachers would have no doubt about their appreciation. Beyond that, they would wow them with small and big surprises.

The project was to begin officially the following Monday. On the Friday before, Tony bounced his basketball into the classroom and rolled it under his desk. Basketball season was about to begin, and he wanted to use every extra minute to get ready.

"Tony, the basketball belongs in your locker or the gym, not in class," said Mr. Newman. "For today, bring it here and I'll keep it for you."

"What?! It's not hurting anything here, Mr. Newman. Please, can I keep it with me?"

"No. You can't," answered the teacher. The other students in the class were listening carefully, waiting to see what Tony would do. They knew how he felt about his basketball.

Tony stayed in his seat, pretending to stare at his pencil. Mr. Newman remained in the front of the room, waiting for Tony to obey. No one made a sound. It was David who broke the silence. "Come on, Tony. Just give it to him."

"Why should I? It's my basketball," answered Tony. It was not like him to disobey, but he did have a temper that sometimes got him into trouble.

"Because he is the teacher and you are the student," said David. "He's not being unreasonable, Tony. You are." David never was afraid to say what he thought.

Tony got up slowly, to everyone's relief, and handed Mr. Newman the basketball. As he did, he said, "Mr. Conroy let me keep it with me last year."

By lunchtime, everyone in the group had heard about Tony's display of disobedience. "This is just great," said David. "Three days before we begin the Be-Good-to-Teacher Week, someone decides to be *bad* to a teacher."

"Knock it off, David," said Tony. "How was I supposed to know that he didn't understand basketball like Mr. Conroy does?" He paused. "Besides, I still say I'm right and I'm going to do it again tomorrow."

---

10 KNOW-IT-ALLS AND LEARN-IT-ALLS

- Opening paragraphs
  - Read together.
  - Instruct students to complete the chart with their own ideas of how each person might respond.
- Chart
  - Discuss first example together, collecting possible answers from students.
  - Students complete chart individually.
  - Circulate, showing your pleasure over their creativity and helping those who need it.
- Verse
  - As students write in the verse, call on various ones to recite it.
  - Insist on expressive recitation.

 SPIN-OFF

DEAR DAVID. Invite students to write to "David" for help with a problem. David will be the pen name of an anonymous boy or girl in your class. Select "David" by drawing a name from a container, letting only "David" know the results of the selection.

---

11 OBEDIENCE: PROJECT SERVANT STORY AND INTERMISSION

- Read trait information.
  - Drill for memory and understanding.
- Story
  - Instruct students to read the story individually, or call on various students to read it to the class.
- Intermission
  - Allow time for students to answer the Intermission question.
  - Discuss answers.
- Follow-up discussion.
  - Use the questions on the following page to discuss and reinforce the principles in the Project Servant story.

 SPIN-OFF

Working Things Out. Follow the principle of working things out by talking them over, as presented in the Project Servant story. Instruct students to team up with a friend to construct situations that would be improved by open discussion between the two or more people involved in it.

Serve your students by modeling obedience.

12 STORY FOLLOW-UP QUESTIONS

- Story follow-up questions.
  1. What statement began the idea for the second Project Servant plan? Who said it? ["I wish we could think of a way to let the teachers know we appreciate them." Henry said it.]
  2. What did the students call their plan? [Be-Good-To-Teacher Week.]
  3. What did Tony do with his basketball, and why did he suddenly show up with it? [He bounced it into the room and rolled it under his desk. Basketball season was about to begin.]
  4. How did Mr. Newman, the students, and Tony react when Mr. Newman instructed Tony to bring the ball to him? [Mr. Newman waited quietly, the students were silent, Tony stared at his pencil. Ultimately he gave the ball to Mr. Newman, but with a poor attitude.]
  5. What was Tony's plan for the following day? [To repeat the scene.]
  6. What evidence is there in the story that Tony thought bringing the basketball into the room would be permissible? [His reference to Mr. Conroy.]
  7. What did the group do in response to Tony's behavior? [Put the project on hold.]
  8. How did Tony's attitude change overnight and what caused the change? [He decided to leave his basketball out of the classroom voluntarily; he had a chance encounter with Mr. Newman at a basketball hoop and was able to work things out.]
  9. What might have been the consequences of Tony's behavior if it had not changed? [Student Choice.]
  10. What does the encounter Tony had with Mr. Newman demonstrate about the value of talking things over? What are some ways this same technique could be applied to families? To churches? To nations? [Student Choice.]

13 PUNCTUALITY

- Read and discuss trait information.
- Complete and discuss page as directed.
  1-2. Briefly share smoke and vinegar experiences.
  3. Look up the word "sluggard" together. Instruct students to write definition. Quiz briefly for understanding.
  4-5. Allow time for students to answer, then call on them to respond.
  6. Use the simile shown on the reduced student page as an example for other similes the students will write. Enjoy the creativity and insight of your students as they complete this exercise.

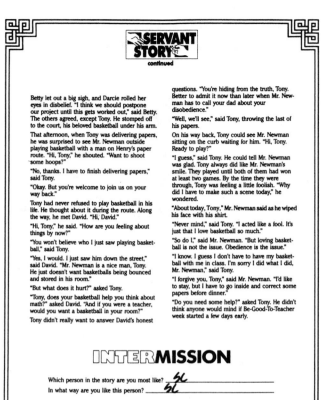

SERVANT STORY continued

Betty let out a big sigh, and Darcie rolled her eyes in disbelief. "I think we should postpone our project until this gets worked out," said Betty. The others agreed, except Tony. He stomped off to the court, his beloved basketball under his arm.

That afternoon, when Tony was delivering papers, he was surprised to see Mr. Newman outside playing basketball with a man on Henry's paper route. "Hi, Tony," he shouted. "Want to shoot some hoops?"

"No, thanks. I have to finish delivering papers," said Tony.

"Okay. But you're welcome to join us on your way back."

Tony had never refused to play basketball in his life. He thought about it during the route. Along the way, he met David. "Hi, David."

"Hi, Tony," he said. "How are you feeling about things by now?"

"You won't believe who I just saw playing basketball," said Tony.

"Yes, I would. I just saw him down the street," said David. "Mr. Newman is a nice man, Tony. He just doesn't want basketballs being bounced and stored in his room."

"But what does it hurt?" asked Tony.

"Tony, does your basketball help you think about math?" asked David. "And if you were a teacher, would you want a basketball in your room?"

Tony didn't really want to answer David's honest questions. "You're hiding from the truth, Tony. Better to admit it now than later when Mr. Newman has to call your dad about your disobedience."

"Well, we'll see," said Tony, throwing the last of his papers.

On his way back, Tony could see Mr. Newman sitting on the curb waiting for him. "Hi, Tony. Ready to play?"

"I guess," said Tony. He could tell Mr. Newman was glad. Tony always did like Mr. Newman's smile. They played until both of them had won at least two games. By the time they were through, Tony was feeling a little foolish. "Why did I have to make such a scene today," he wondered.

"About today, Tony," Mr. Newman said as he wiped his face with his shirt.

"Never mind," said Tony. "I acted like a fool. It's just that I love basketball so much."

"So do I," said Mr. Newman. "But loving basketball is not the issue. Obedience is the issue."

"I know. I guess I don't have to have my basketball with me in class. I'm sorry I did what I did, Mr. Newman," said Tony.

"I forgive you, Tony," said Mr. Newman. "I'd like to stay, but I have to go inside and correct some papers before dinner."

"Do you need some help?" asked Tony. He didn't think anyone would mind if Be-Good-To-Teacher week started a few days early.

INTERMISSION

Which person in the story are you most like? _S.C._

In what way are you like this person? _S.C._

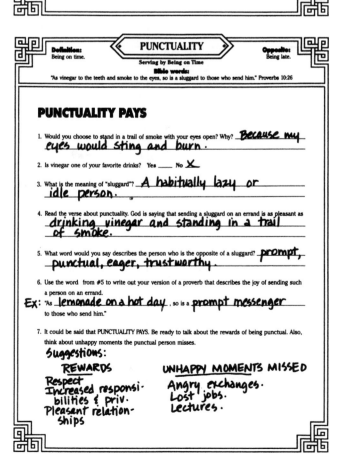

Definition: Being on time.

◇ PUNCTUALITY ◇

Serving by Being on Time

Opposite: Being late.

Bible words:
"As vinegar to the teeth and smoke to the eyes, so is a sluggard to those who send him." Proverbs 10:26

PUNCTUALITY PAYS

1. Would you choose to stand in a trail of smoke with your eyes open? Why? _Because my eyes would sting and burn._

2. Is vinegar one of your favorite drinks? Yes ___ No _X_

3. What is the meaning of "sluggard"? _A habitually lazy or idle person._

4. Read the verse about punctuality. God is saying that sending a sluggard on an errand is as pleasant as _drinking vinegar and standing in a trail of smoke._

5. What word would you say describes the person who is the opposite of a sluggard? _prompt, punctual, eager, trustworthy._

6. Use the word from #5 to write out your version of a proverb that describes the joy of sending such a person on an errand.

Ex: "As _lemonade on a hot day_, so is a _prompt messenger_ to those who send him."

7. It could be said that PUNCTUALITY PAYS. Be ready to talk about the rewards of being punctual. Also, think about unhappy moments the punctual person misses.

Suggestions:

REWARDS	UNHAPPY MOMENTS MISSED
Respect	Angry exchanges.
Increased responsibilities & priv.	Lost jobs.
Pleasant relationships	Lectures.

22

PROMPT AND NOT-SO-PROMPT

Darcie moaned loudly when Mr. Black asked the class to turn in their book reports. Hers was undone and at home under a stack of snapshots of last summer's vacation. What do you think Darcie might have been doing instead of writing her book report? *Looking at the pictures.*

Tony spun around the corner just as the class was saying "with liberty and justice for all." "At least I made it before they finished the flag salute," he thought. What do you think was the reason for Tony's frequent tardiness? *Got up late; moved slowly; talked with friends.*

Betty, David, and Henry also had areas of their lives that were prompt and not-so-prompt. We all do unless we learn punctuality. On this chart, design a schedule that you believe is reasonable for a sixth grader to follow. Include time for each of the activities listed below the chart.

PUNCTUALITY PLAN

ACTIVITY	TIME
Before School: *6c*	
After School: *6c*	

ACTIVITIES: Time with God   Homework   Preparing for school   Relaxation
Chores   Mealtime   Room straightened

PUNCTUALITY PUZZLER: In what New Testament story was Jesus accused of being late? *Mary and Martha felt their brother, Lazarus, would have lived if Jesus had arrived earlier. (John 11)*

King Xerxes is furious over Vashti's disobedience.

NOTE: You may wish to ask each student to write his/her simile on a sheet of paper for your files.

7. Discuss benefits of being punctual. Consider the unhappy moments, such as irritated parents, that a punctual person misses.

Serve your students by being on time with plans, activities, and praise.

14 PROMPT AND NOT-SO-PROMPT

- Read each paragraph, comparing answers.
- Punctuality Plan.
  ◗ Explain the chart.
  ◗ Provide examples, as needed.
  ◗ Circulate as students design their plan.
- Punctuality Puzzler
  ◗ Discuss and come to an answer now or turn the puzzler into a mystery question that will be answered tomorrow. You may wish to give the person who answers correctly the privilege of writing another puzzler for the class.
  Answer: Story of Mary, Martha, and Lazarus.

 SPIN-OFF

PUNCTUALITY PLAN ACTIVATED. For one week, students try to keep the schedule they have designed. Make adjustments until a realistic schedule emerges. Follow up in another week by asking for progress reports.

15 ESTHER ILLUSTRATION

- Study the picture and discuss.
  ◗ Note the emotions on the king's face.
  ◗ Imagine being there with him.
  ◗ Ask, "If you were in this picture, where and who would you be?"

Study the language of gentleness;
refuse words that bite
and tunes that clash.

16 BACKFIRE: Episode One Of The Esther Story

● Introduce the story by emphasizing the fact that in ancient times kings were all-powerful. You had to do what they told you or suffer the consequences (usually death!). Prepare the class for Vashti's refusal by telling them that King Xerxes was one of the most powerful kings in all the world.

◗ After students have read the story, discuss the reasons for Vashti's refusal and the consequences of this bold act. It is generally agreed that Xerxes' request connotated more than a simple appearance of the queen at the banquet. The reputation of such banquets suggests strongly that Vashti was being asked to do something that at the very least would be embarrassing to her and at the most would be immoral.

◗ Elicit thoughtful student responses by asking the questions – "What is one thing **you** would refuse to do if asked by someone in leadership over you? Why would you refuse to do it?"

◗ Lay groundwork for the Back to Backfire review page by asking some of the more difficult questions in modified form. For example, you might ask question 4 in this way – "What thoughts might have gone through Vashti's mind as she tried to decide what to do about the king's request?"

17 BACK TO BACKFIRE

● Instruct students to complete the page carefully and thoughtfully, answering in complete sentences.

◗ As you circulate for praise and reinforcement, make mental note of some of the best answers for later sharing and discussion with the class.

SPIN-OFF

SAYING NO WHEN IT HURTS. Do a mini-unit on obedience and disobedience. When should our obedience to God take precedence over other levels of obedience? Discuss "following our conscience."

The Project Servant suggestions for this unit may be found on page 88 of this book.

EPISODE ONE

BACK FIRE

ESTHER

King Xerxes had been showing off his wealth and majesty to the leaders of the land for 180 days, and now he wanted to end it with a week-long banquet.

He chose to hold the splendid affair in the enclosed garden. Lovely blue and white banners hung from silver rings attached to marble pillars. Gold and silver couches were arranged in a festive way on a floor of costly stones, and each guest was served the wine of his choice in a gold goblet with its own design. The king loved to be generous, and it showed.

After seven days of eating and drinking, King Xerxes' drunk mind came up with an idea. "Servants, tell Vashti to prepare herself! I want to display her beauty to my guests!"

At the same time the king was giving his banquet, Queen Vashti was giving a party for the women of the palace. When the servants brought her the message from the king, she stubbornly refused. "I will not do this!" she said. Vashti knew what kinds of wrong things women were asked to do in front of drunken men at banquets. The women were shocked! It was not an everyday thing to disobey an order from the king.

The servants carried her message back to King Xerxes. When he heard it, he burned with anger. He felt embarrassed in front of his friends because his wife had refused to obey him. "I must do something to show everyone that she cannot get away with this," he thought, with muddled mind.

He needed advice from experts of the law to tell him what he could do to Vashti. "What shall I do to Vashti for disobeying my command?" he asked.

The men were close friends of the king and shared his horror at what had happened. One friend spoke up and said, "Vashti not only did wrong against you, she did wrong against all of us. When our wives find out that the queen disobeyed you, they will disobey us. They will say, 'If Vashti does it, so can I!' He added, "There will be no end to the disrespect and discord in our homes!"

All of the men agreed, and their worried whispers floated in and out around the blasts of fury from the king. "What you should do," said Memucan, "is issue a decree that can never be changed. It should say that Vashti can never again enter the presence of the king and that she will be replaced as your queen. By doing this, all of the women of the kingdom will be forced to respect their husbands!"

The men and the king agreed that this was an excellent idea. King Xerxes ordered the decree to be written in the language of every province. It was delivered immediately and proclaimed that every man was to be ruler over his own household.

No decree, however, could remove the memory of the day the queen refused the king's command and put a sour ending on his party.

BACK TO BACK FIRE

BACKFIRE 1

1. What were some of the things that King Xerxes did to make his week-long banquet special?
   Decorated the indoor garden; served quality wine in personal gold goblets.

2. What idea did he come up with after seven days of eating and drinking?
   To display Queen Vashti to his drunk friends.

3. How did Vashti respond to the king's request?
   She refused (probably knowing what it would lead to).

4. What emotions do you think Vashti felt as she considered her response to the king?
   Perhaps mixed: wanted to obey the king, yet desired to maintain personal respect. Also, fear.

5. Do you believe that Vashti was right in disobeying the king?
   SC

6. Put yourself in King Xerxes' place. What would you have done to Vashti in this situation?
   SC

7. Pretend you are listening to the king's advisors discussing their own fears. What are some of the things you might hear?
   "Our wives might copy her!" "All of the women might rebel."

8. Identify any parts of the story that show wisdom or foolishness.
   SC

NEXT-TIME NOTES
to make next time better

SP 8:

SP 9:

SP 10:

SP 11:

SP 12:

SP 13:

SP 14:

SP 15:

SP 16:

SP 17:

Project Servant:

Other:

AFTERTHOUGHTS
Thoughts too good to lose • Kidquotes • Thoughts from God • Ideas

STEP ONE

A pastor greeted a young husband with "How are you?" The young man tossed aside the expected "Just fine," for the truth: He had failed an exam that morning, his wife was suffering from a serious bout with the flu, and his paycheck was late. The pastor, pretending to listen, said, "That's great!" and moved on to someone else. The young man had reason to feel that he had been treated unkindly. Not listening to what another person is saying is rude.

Listening, on the other hand, is kind. There are at least three reasons Christian teachers must demonstrate this kindness to their students:

1. Listening helps us evaluate the progress of our students. As a tongue twister says, "Listeners learn lasting lessons." The lessons learned by a listening teacher are invaluable in assessing the progress and needs of our students. The wise teacher understands that listening "between the lines" is as important as listening to right and wrong answers.

2. Listening validates the importance of the speaker. For most of us, it takes courage to wrap our thoughts in words and send them out to a potential listener. If the listener receives our word-wrapped thoughts with respect, we are encouraged to try again. We are helped to believe that our thoughts matter and that we matter. Like the young man mentioned above, children learn quickly whether or not their words matter to the listener. We possess the power, by the very way we listen, to confirm the value of our students.

3. Listening enables us to accurately model the behavior of God. This must not be understated. Without ever really being heard by a godly leader, we make faith in an attentive God more difficult for our students. Listening to our students can, in a real way, lead them to faith in the attentive, listening God.

PATTERNING

Challenge yourself to become a better listener than you now are. Needless to say, if God were graded on His listening skills, He would get an A+. What about you? What grade would your students give you? What grade would your family give you? Your friends?

Here are some tips to help you strengthen your listening skills:

- Consciously set aside other thoughts and determine to hear what the speaker is saying.
- Maintain frequent eye contact.
- Ask God to help you hear what is really being said and respond correctly.
- Throw away "pat" comebacks to classroom discussions, such as saying "very good" in response to every answer.
- Follow up a conversation at a later time with a question or comment about it.

Patterning God's attentiveness is no small task, but neither is it of small consequence.

CHEWABLES
Bite-sized thoughts from God's Word

Select a thought to "chew on" during this unit:

"In the morning, O Lord, You hear my voice; in the morning I lay my requests before You and wait in expectation."   Psalm 5:3

"The Lord would speak to Moses face to face, as a man speaks with his friend."   Exodus 33:11

"These (trials) have come so that your faith – of greater worth than gold, which perishes even though refined by fire – may be proved genuine and may result in praise, glory and honor when Jesus Christ is revealed."   I Peter 1:7

UNIT INFORMATION

Theme Verse:
"Practice hospitality." Romans 12:13

Esther Study:
Esther prepares to see the king, winning the heart of the eunuch in charge of the girls. Mordecai keeps closely in touch with her.

PART A: ATTENTIVENESS

Purpose:
To encourage students to pay more attention to their own faults than those of others.
To show Jesus' feelings toward hypocrites.

Approach:
Everyone has faults.
Jesus can help us with our faults.
He is unhappy when a person only pays attention to the faults of others.

Definition:
Watching and listening closely to what is happening.

Opposite:
Neglecting to notice what is happening.

Trait Verse:
Luke 6:41, 42
"Why do you look at the speck of sawdust in your brother's eye and pay no attention to the plank in your own eye? How can you say to your brother, 'Brother, let me take the speck out of your eye,' when you yourself fail to see the plank in your own eye? You hypocrite, first take the plank out of your eye, and then you will see clearly to remove the speck from your brother's eye."

Visual Reinforcement:
On the day you begin the attentiveness section of the unit, write the following riddle on the chalkboard: "When does a plank look like a speck of sawdust and a speck of sawdust look like a plank?" [When the plank is in your own eye.] Use the riddle to generate interest in the words of Jesus regarding the attitude of the Pharisees.

Enlarge the illustration from SP 20. Place it and the list of Pharisee-style rules from "Ideas" below, on a bulletin board. Overlay both the picture and the list with a sash-type copy of the trait verse.

Ideas:
Using the examples of Tony and Peter from SP 19, ask students to team up to provide the class with a similar example of blocked vision, i.e., of seeing someone else's fault as a plank and your own as a speck of sawdust. If desired, instruct students to write their examples on an actual plank which you bring to class.

To illustrate the heavy load caused by unfair rules, lead the class in transforming the short list of necessary classroom guidelines into a lengthy Pharisee-style list of unnecessary rules.

Use as Desired:
SP 18, Courteous Hospitality
SP 20, A Heavy Load

PART B: FAITH

Purpose:
To present faith as the key to God's help.
To offer examples of how faith might work in the life of a sixth grader.

Approach:
God is pleased when I trust Him.
The same God who helped Bible people will help me when I place my faith in Him.

Definition:
Believing God will do what He says He will do.

Opposite:
Disbelieving God.

Trait Verse:
Hebrews 11:32-34
"And what more shall I say? I do not have time to tell about Gideon, Barak, Samson, Jephthah, David, Samuel, and the prophets, who through faith conquered kingdoms, administered justice, and gained what was promised; who shut the mouths of lions, quenched the fury of the flames, and escaped the edge of the sword; whose weakness was turned to strength; and who became powerful in battle and routed foreign armies."

Visual Reinforcement:
Instruct students to visualize the heroes mentioned in the trait verse. This could be during art or as an independent activity during seatwork. Use the results as a bulletin board. Request a qualified student printer to label each picture and to cut out or write the title, "Weakness Turned to Strength by Faith."

Ideas:
As a class, compose your own version of Hebrews 11:32-34. Use examples of contemporary faith. Post it under a printed copy of the original verse.

Use as Desired:
SP 25, Trusting God Means . . .

PART C: CONFIDENCE

Purpose:
To present an example of one boy's struggle with confidence.

Approach:
God is ready to help His children.

Definition:
A strong belief in the ability of a person or thing.

Opposite:
A strong doubt about the ability of a person or thing.

Trait Verse:
Hebrews 13:6-8. (See verse sheet.)

Visual Reinforcement:
Use a crutch to remind students of Henry's fears in walking on the leg he had broken. Mount it on a bulletin board horizontally, writing the trait information on the background paper inside of the spaces created by the slats and bars of the crutch. Surround the crutch with student work from the unit.

Ideas:
Hold a Fear and Faith Forum. Lead students and a group of parents or other adults in a forum about common fears. Use it as a way to help students and parents understand one another. Mix students and adults into small groups to pray in faith for God's help with the various fears. Close with a pre-rehearsed reading of Hebrews 11 by some students.

Use as Desired:
TG 89, Project Servant: Confidence Through New Challenges

MY PLAN FOR THIS UNIT

_____

_____

_____

_____

18 INTRO TO UNIT

- Read through information together.
  - ▶ Briefly discuss the meaning and practice of hospitality. Ex: Whom do you know who is especially good at hospitality and why?
- Instruct students to begin inking in the design.
- Read Luke 10:38-41 and John 12:1-3 as they begin.
  - ▶ Discuss these examples of hospitality.
  - ▶ Imagine together having Jesus as a dinner guest. What would they serve Him?
  - ▶ Present the idea that some families actually set a place at the table for Jesus, to remind themselves that He is there as "the unseen guest."
  - ▶ Note that serving others through hospitality is really serving Jesus.
- Admire student work and close the session, if you wish, with a hospitable treat.

 SPIN-OFF

COURTEOUS HOSPITALITY. Lead students in a simple or elaborate study of basic manners of entertaining. Present the correct way to make introductions, shake hands, and use dining utensils. Cap the unit with a formal lunch, using authentic tableware and luncheon food or improvising.

---

19 BLOCKED VISION

- Read through page together.
  - ▶ Stop to discuss and explain as desired.
  - ▶ Stress the strong feelings of Jesus toward hypocrisy.
  - ▶ Discuss hypocrisy: Its meaning, its behavior.
- The Pharisees
  - ▶ Complete the chart together or individually.
  - ▶ You may wish to divide your class into teams of 2 or 3 students each. Assign each team a section to look up and analyze.

Serve your students by paying attention to their good qualities.

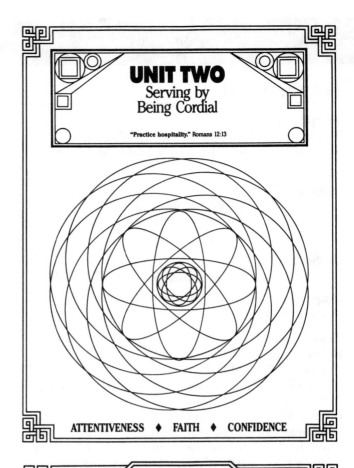

UNIT TWO
Serving by
Being Cordial

"Practice hospitality." Romans 12:13

ATTENTIVENESS ◆ FAITH ◆ CONFIDENCE

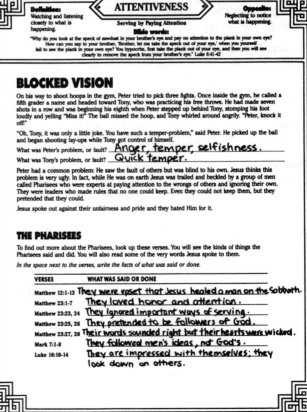

Definition:	◆ ATTENTIVENESS ◆	Opposite:
Watching and listening closely to what is happening.	Serving by Paying Attention	Neglecting to notice what is happening.

Bible words:
"Why do you look at the speck of sawdust in your brother's eye and pay no attention to the plank in your own eye? How can you say to your brother, 'Brother, let me take the speck out of your eye,' when you yourself fail to see the plank in your own eye? You hypocrite, first take the plank out of your eye, and then you will see clearly to remove the speck from your brother's eye." Luke 6:41-42

BLOCKED VISION

On his way to shoot hoops in the gym, Peter tried to pick three fights. Once inside the gym, he called a fifth grader a name and headed toward Tony, who was practicing his free throws. He had made seven shots in a row and was beginning his eighth when Peter stepped up behind Tony, stomping his foot loudly and yelling "Miss it!" The ball missed the hoop, and Tony whirled around angrily. "Peter, knock it off!"

"Oh, Tony, it was only a little joke. You have such a temper-problem," said Peter. He picked up the ball and began shooting lay-ups while Tony got control of himself.

What was Peter's problem, or fault? <u>Anger, temper, selfishness.</u>

What was Tony's problem, or fault? <u>Quick temper.</u>

Peter had a common problem: He saw the fault of others but was blind to his own. Jesus thinks this problem is very ugly. In fact, while He was on earth Jesus was trailed and heckled by a group of men called Pharisees who were experts at paying attention to the wrongs of others and ignoring their own. They were leaders who made rules that no one could keep. Even they could not keep them, but they pretended that they could.

Jesus spoke out against their unfairness and pride and they hated Him for it.

THE PHARISEES

To find out more about the Pharisees, look up these verses. You will see the kinds of things the Pharisees said and did. You will also read some of the very words Jesus spoke to them.

In the space next to the verses, write the facts of what was said or done.

VERSES	WHAT WAS SAID OR DONE
Matthew 12:1-13	<u>They were upset that Jesus healed a man on the Sabbath.</u>
Matthew 23:1-7	<u>They loved honor and attention.</u>
Matthew 23:23, 24	<u>They ignored important ways of serving.</u>
Matthew 23:25, 26	<u>They pretended to be followers of God.</u>
Matthew 23:27, 28	<u>Their words sounded right but their hearts were wicked.</u>
Mark 7:1-8	<u>They followed men's ideas, not God's.</u>
Luke 18:10-14	<u>They are impressed with themselves; they look down on others.</u>

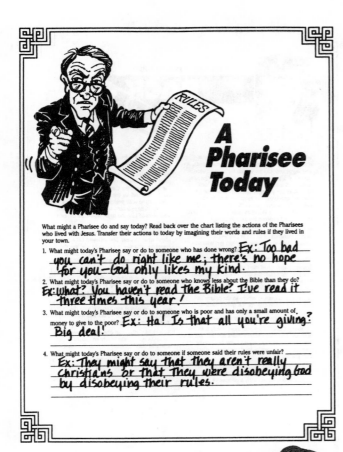

What might a Pharisee do and say today? Read back over the chart listing the actions of the Pharisees who lived with Jesus. Transfer their actions to today by imagining their words and rules if they lived in your town.

1. What might today's Pharisee say or do to someone who has done wrong? Ex: Too bad you can't do right like me; there's no hope for you—God only likes my kind.

2. What might today's Pharisee say or do to someone who knows less about the Bible than they do? Ex: What? You haven't read The Bible? I've read it three times this year!

3. What might today's Pharisee say or do to someone who is poor and has only a small amount of money to give to the poor? Ex: Ha! Is that all you're giving? Big deal!

4. What might today's Pharisee say or do to someone if someone said their rules were unfair? Ex: They might say that they aren't really christians or that they were disobeying God by disobeying their rules.

20 A PHARISEE TODAY

- Study and comment on the illustration.
  ◗ Call on students to describe the person in the illustration.
- Assist students in translating the behavior of Bible Pharisees to today's world.
  ◗ Pick out the main point of each of the entries on the chart on page 19. Apply its principle to life today.
  ◗ Encourage students to stretch their minds to meet the challenges of the exercise.
  ◗ Ask, "Do you think Jesus' opinion of fault-finding has changed?"
- Identify signs of hypocrisy in areas of life other than religion.

SPIN-OFF
A HEAVY LOAD. Post examples of some of the more "heavy loaded" rules of the Pharisees. The following books may help you: UNDERSTANDING THE TALMUD by Ernest R. Trattner; THE EVERYMAN'S TALMUD by Rev. Dr. A. Cohen; FROM BIBLE TO MISHNA by J. Weingreen.

---

21 ESTHER ILLUSTRATION

- Study and discuss the picture.
  ◗ Construct with your students conversations which could have been spoken by various groups of people in the Esther stories. Suggestions follow.
- Conversation ideas
  1. Between Esther and Mordecai.
  2. Between two women who had been at Vashti's party.
  3. Between two young girls who were hoping to be chosen to go to the palace.
  4. Between an official who had been at Xerxes' banquet and his wife who had stayed at home.

A search for the new queen begins.

22 BACKFIRE: Episode Two Of The Esther Story

- Instruct students to read the story.
  ◆ If reading it aloud, insist on good expression by the readers.

 SPIN-OFF

QUEEN HUNT. Lead your class in compiling a Job Description sheet for the position of queen. Write it as if King Xerxes had composed it himself. This will be valuable in discerning the image students have so far of Xerxes.

ESTHER

EPISODE TWO

BACK FIRE

When the king got over the shock of Vashti's refusal to display herself in front of his friends, it was suggested that he search for a new queen. "Let's put a person in every province of the kingdom," said a friend of the king. "He will look over all of the young women in his section of the land and bring the most beautiful to the palace. The young woman that pleases you the most will replace Vashti as queen." The king liked the idea and ordered the search to begin.

In the city of Susa, the chairman of the beauty search gathered all of the young women together. Among them was Esther, a Jewish girl who was lovely in every way. Esther was her Persian name. Her real name was Hadassah.

Esther's parents had died when she was young. She grew up under the care of her cousin Mordecai, a fine man who worked as an officer in the household of King Xerxes.

Esther was chosen to return to the palace as one of the candidates for the queen contest. Hegai was the leader of the team who would prepare the girls for their visit with the king. He thought that Esther was more lovely than the rest, and he quickly began taking special care of her. He ordered her maids to give her beauty treatments and special food, and gave Esther the best place to stay.

Mordecai must have missed having Esther at home with him. He walked past the courtyard every day hoping to catch a glimpse of her or perhaps speak a few words. She often sent messages to him with one of her maids.

All of the girls in the queen contest had to complete twelve months of beauty treatments. For the first six months they were treated with oil and myrrh, and for the second six months they were treated with perfumes and cosmetics. Each girl would have a turn with the king. The girl who pleased him the most would be the new queen.

When it was Esther's turn, Hegai gave her advice about what to wear. She followed his advice, and everyone who saw her thought she was the loveliest girl of all. The king agreed and pronounced Esther queen instead of Vashti.

King Xerxes set a royal crown on Esther's head and then gave a great banquet in her honor. He gave everyone a holiday and gave them gifts.

One of the first things Esther did as queen was tell the king about two men who had plotted to kill him. Mordecai was the one who discovered their plans, and his loyal act was written down in the record book of the king.

As a child, Esther had obeyed and loved Mordecai. As queen, she wisely continued in her love and obedience toward him. She must have felt very proud of his bravery, and he must have been equally pleased with her success as queen.

22

---

23 BACK TO BACKFIRE

- Instruct students to complete the questions.
- Discuss one or two issues from the story that you feel are of special interest to your students.
  ◆ Call for comments or questions about the story after the page is completed.

BACK TO BACK FIRE

BACKFIRE 2

1. How was King Xerxes going to select a new queen?
   By gathering young girls from the kingdom and choosing one to be queen.

2. What were some of the details of Esther's life presented in this story?
   She lived in Susa, she was pretty, her real name was Hadassah, she was adopted by her cousin Mordecai.

3. Who was the leader of the queen-to-be preparation team and what did he do to prepare the girls for the contest?
   Hegai was in charge of the girls. They had 12 months of beauty treatments of oil and cosmetics.

4. How was Esther's attentiveness important to her being chosen by the king?
   She listened to and followed Hegai's advice.

5. What was one of the first things Esther did as queen? What does this tell you about Esther's character?
   She told the king about a plot to kill him. She was loyal, she was brave, she loved Mordecai.

6. How did Esther display obedience in this story?
   She continued to listen to Mordecai; also followed instructions of Hegai.

7. Put yourself in the place of King Xerxes. What qualities would you have looked for in a girl trying to be your queen?
   SL

23

> Character is a diamond
> that scratches every other stone.

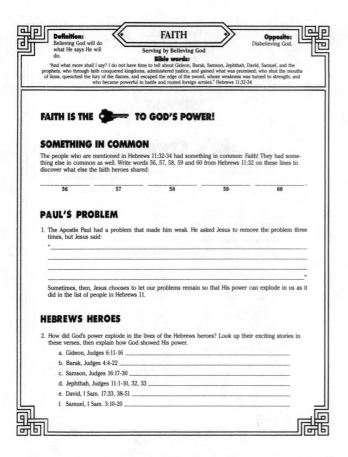

Definition:
Believing God will do what He says He will do.

FAITH

Opposite:
Disbelieving God.

Serving by Believing God

Bible words:
"And what more shall I say? I do not have time to tell about Gideon, Barak, Samson, Jephthah, David, Samuel, and the prophets, who through faith conquered kingdoms, administered justice, and gained what was promised; who shut the mouths of lions, quenched the fury of the flames, and escaped the edge of the sword; whose weakness was turned to strength; and who became powerful in battle and routed foreign armies." Hebrews 11:32-34

FAITH IS THE 🔑 TO GOD'S POWER!

SOMETHING IN COMMON

The people who are mentioned in Hebrews 11:32-34 had something in common: Faith! They had something else in common as well. Write words 56, 57, 58, 59 and 60 from Hebrews 11:32 on these lines to discover what else the faith heroes shared:

_____ _____ _____ _____ _____
56   57   58   59   60

PAUL'S PROBLEM

1. The Apostle Paul had a problem that made him weak. He asked Jesus to remove the problem three times, but Jesus said:

"_____
_____
_____

Sometimes, then, Jesus chooses to let our problems remain so that His power can explode in us as it did in the list of people in Hebrews 11.

HEBREWS HEROES

2. How did God's power explode in the lives of the Hebrews heroes? Look up their exciting stories in these verses, then explain how God showed His power.

   a. Gideon, Judges 6:11-16 _____
   b. Barak, Judges 4:4-22 _____
   c. Samson, Judges 16:17-30 _____
   d. Jephthah, Judges 11:1-10, 32, 33 _____
   e. David, I Sam. 17:33, 38-51 _____
   f. Samuel, I Sam. 3:10-20 _____

Faith is out of sight!

God loves faith! In fact, He says that it is impossible to please Him without faith! (Read it for yourself in Hebrews 11:6.) When we put our faith, or trust, in God, we are telling Him that we believe He will take care of us in the best way.

TRUST GOD
Match these examples of faith.

1. David shows faith when he studies for a test, then . . .
2. Henry shows faith when he promises to try to earn money, then . . .
3. Darcie shows faith when she asks God to help her be friendly, then . . .
4. Tony shows faith by admitting to God that he has let his anger get out of control, then . . .
5. Betty shows faith when she is afraid at night, then . . .

. . . trusts God to help him find a part-time job.
. . . trusts God to forgive him.
. . . trusts God to keep her safe.
. . . trusts God to remind him of the correct answer.
. . . trusts Him to give her people to befriend.

How has someone you know shown faith?

24 FAITH

- Something in Common
  - ◗ Read the verses.
  - ◗ Students count out the words, and enter words #56-60.
  - ◗ Note that God's way of looking at our weakness is not the way we look at it. He sees it as a possibility for power!
- Paul's problem
  - ◗ Call on a student to read I Cor. 12:9 to the class.
  - ◗ Enter the quote onto the lines.
  - ◗ Discuss the idea of power exploding through our weaknesses and God's use of them to show Himself through us.
- Hebrews Heroes
  - ◗ Assign a section of verses to various students to read out loud.
  - ◗ Students enter their ideas after the text is read.
  - ◗ Discuss each, helping students imagine being the person receiving the power.

Serve your students by teaching them with faith.

25 GOD LOVES FAITH!

- Build up God's love of faith.
  - ◗ Discuss what faith means to Him, as mentioned in the paragraph.
- Trust God.
  - ◗ Students match examples of faith.
  - ◗ Discuss each and help students apply the principles to their own lives.
  - ◗ Solicit examples of students' experience with faith, as well as experiences of those they know.

■ SPIN-OFF

TRUSTING GOD MEANS . . . Collect students' own versions of "Trusting God Means . . ." Make a book of them. Ask a student to design a cover of heavy paper, then ask the librarian to bind it for you.

26 CONFIDENCE: PROJECT SERVANT STORY AND INTERMISSION

- Present trait information.
  - Drill and review this and past traits, and theme verses.
- Instruct students to read the story.
  - Quiz briefly for general comprehension.
- Intermission
  - Discuss, considering the many ways people handle their fears.
  - Point out that often our pattern of handling fears is set in childhood. This makes it critical that children learn the correct way of dealing with fear and faith.

27 PROJECT SERVANT STORY AND FOLLOW-UP QUESTIONS

- Use the following questions to reinforce the story and stimulate thinking about its principles.
  1. What was the nightmare that plagued Henry? [That he would re-break his leg after the cast was removed.]
  2. What were Henry's other fears? [What if it hurt; what if I limp; what if it looks different than my other one.]
  3. What did Dr. Simmons expect Henry to do? [Exercise; begin walking soon without crutches.]
  4. How did Henry feel about his fears? [Embarrassed; called them "silly."]
  5. What might Henry have been doing or saying unknowingly that enabled the group to sense his fears? [Student opinion. Suggestions: body language, tone of voice.]
  6. What did each member of the group do to quietly give Henry confidence? [Tony related an experience of his neighbor; David helped with his exercises; Betty gave an oral report on broken bones; Darcie subtly challenged him to be walking without crutches for the field trip.]
  7. How might this experience help Henry in the future? [Student opinion.]
  8. What if the group had thought of ways of helping Henry but chose not to carry them out? How would Henry's recovery had been different? [Student opinion.]

The Project Servant suggestions for this unit may be found on page 89 of this book.

| **Definition:** A strong belief in the ability of a person or thing. | **CONFIDENCE** Serving by Expecting the Best | **Opposite:** Doubting the abilities of a person or thing. |

Bible words:
"So we say with confidence, 'The Lord is my helper; I will not be afraid. What can man do to me?' Remember your leaders, who spoke the word of God to you. Consider the outcome of their way of life and imitate their faith. Jesus Christ is the same yesterday and today and forever." Hebrews 13:6-8

It's Over!

The same nightmare woke Henry up three times in one night. In it, the doctor would remove his cast and everyone would cheer. They would then beg Henry to walk without his crutches. But when he would step down on his leg, it would break again.

The nightmares frightened Henry. It made him wish that the doctor was not removing his cast right after breakfast that morning. "What if my nightmare comes true?"

Other fears joined the first. "What if it hurts a lot?" "What if I have a limp?" "What if my broken leg looks different than the other one?" By the time Henry arrived at the doctor's office, he had a large collection of fears waiting to rob him of the happiness at having the itchy cast removed.

Dr. Simmons worked quickly and gently. At any minute, Henry would see his leg for the first time in six weeks. "I hope I recognize it," he thought. At first, Henry would only peek at his leg. "It looks familiar," he thought. "Maybe a little pale, but it matches my other one." Relief chased one of his fears away, but the others hung around to bother him.

Dr. Simmons gave Henry instructions and a list of exercises to do every day. "Use the crutches until you feel confident about walking again."

"He'll be walking in no time," said Mr. Klinkdale. He had taken the morning off so that he could be with Henry at the doctor's office. "I know he will," said Dr. Simmons.

Henry was embarrassed by his silly fears. If he had talked about them to someone, he would have found out that his fears were normal. Instead, Henry decided he wouldn't tell anyone about them except God. Henry had trusted Him for other things, so he knew God would help him with this, too.

"Hey, Henry, your leg looks good." Tony had caught up with him in the hall. "The people on your paper route are going to be happy to see you back soon."

Henry didn't know what to say, so he just smiled. He missed the people on his paper route, too, but pedaling a bike might hurt a leg that has been broken.

"Well, look at you, Henry Klinkdale," said Mrs. Maddux. "It looks like you'll be back in PE soon. I'm glad for you, but I will surely miss your help." Henry and Mrs. Maddux had become good friends.

"Henry!" yelled Betty and Darcie. "Wait up for us." They had just gotten off their bus. "Let us see your leg."

"Oh, I miss seeing my signature on your cast. Do you mind if I write on your leg?" Darcie asked with a giggle.

Henry walked with them to class. He believed that he had kept his fears from showing in front of his friends, but he was wrong. All of them noticed.

"I think something is wrong with Henry," said Betty. She had a warm heart toward people in need.

The others agreed. "I think he's afraid to walk on his leg. That's what happened to my neighbor when she broke her leg."

"Well, then, we'd better do what we can to help him," said David, getting out his pencil.

"We don't need a print-out on this one, David," said Betty. "We just need common sense." Each of them chose one thing to do for Henry.

That afternoon Tony walked home with Henry. "You know, when my neighbor broke her leg, she was afraid to walk on it. She was afraid it would break again. Her doctor said that's a normal feeling."

"Really?" said Henry. "That's interesting." Inside himself, Henry was much more interested than he was letting on and Tony knew it.

Two days later, Betty gave an oral report on broken bones and how strong they heal. Henry paid more attention to her report than any of the others that were given that day.

David dropped by Henry's house and asked him if he would show him the exercises he did every day. Henry hadn't done them for two days, so David's visit made Henry's mother very happy. "Come back anytime," she said as David left. The next day and every other day for a week he helped Henry with his exercises.

"Henry! The field trip to the science center is in one week," said Darcie. "It's too bad you'll have to go with your crutches. Oh well, you'll still have fun."

The group checked up on Henry's progress often. "It's going to be so great to see him without those pesky crutches," said Darcie. "Yes, but when," said David.

The night before the field trip, Henry decided to try to walk normally around his room. His old fears tried to keep him from it, but Henry chose not to pay attention to them. With a deep breath, Henry got up and pretended that both legs were strong. By the time he got to the door, he realized that he wasn't pretending. Both legs were strong!

The phone rang and, without thinking, Henry ran to answer it. His family stopped what they were doing to stare at Henry. Their wide eyes made Henry laugh. "It's for you, Mom," said Henry. She came to the phone wiping her wet cheeks. The last time Henry had seen her cry was the day he had been hit by the car. That was all behind him now.

That night Henry kept waking up, but not because of nightmares. Henry's mind was feeding him pictures of his happy friends. He imagined seeing their faces when he hopped off the bus without his crutches. God had helped Henry walk by putting people around him to give him confidence.

When Henry finally fell asleep, it was with a grin on his lips and a hand on his strong leg.

INTER**MISSION**

In what other ways could Henry have handled his fears?

NEXT-TIME NOTES
to make next time better

SP 18:

SP 19:

SP 20:

SP 21:

SP 22:

SP 23:

SP 24:

SP 25:

SP 26:

SP 27:

PROJECT SERVANT:

OTHER:

AFTERTHOUGHTS
Thoughts too good to lose • Kidquotes • Thoughts from God • Ideas

STEP ONE

There sits Jennifer. Bouncy ponytails, polka-dot ribbons tied just right, sent from a home that is trying to follow God's plan for their family. Next to her sits Todd. No socks on his feet or laces in his shoes, sent from a home that runs on empty. And here sits me, ready to begin a unit on Thankfulness. What mutuality do these two extremes share? How can I neutralize their differences and give them each an equal opportunity at being thankful?

I will let God be their neutralizer. He will be their meeting ground, their mutual focus of gratitude. Together, we will celebrate God.

We will celebrate His creativity. We will enjoy His colors, His music, His design.

We will celebrate His genius. We will marvel at His ability to orchestrate the universe while giving a baby its first breath.

We will celebrate His character by considering His enduring love and kindness.

We will celebrate His Word by cementing parts of it in our minds.

Yes, a celebration of God is the great meeting ground of His children, eliminating man-made barriers of age, class, and whether or not there are socks on our feet.

PATTERNING

God will one day give a word of praise to each of His children. With this in mind, write out one word of praise for each of your students. Choose a way to let them hear it as a group or individually.

CHEWABLES
Bite-sized thoughts from God's Word.

Select a thought to "chew-on" during this unit:

"But thanks be to God, who always leads us in triumphal procession in Christ and through us spreads everywhere the fragrance of the knowledge of Him."
2 Corinthians 2:14

"I will sing to the Lord, for He has been good to me."
Psalm 13:6

"I will praise the Lord, who counsels me; even at night my heart instructs me."
Psalm 16:7

UNIT INFORMATION

Theme Verse:
"Bless those who persecute you; bless, and do not curse." Rom. 12:14

Esther Study:
Mordecai refuses to bow to Haman.

PART A: THANKFULNESS

Purpose:
To generate an appreciation for God by leading the students through a close look at it.
To provide the students with an imaginative exercise in demonstrating that appreciation.

Approach:
I can show my appreciation of God in many special ways.

Definition:
Being glad for the goodness of God and others.

Opposite:
Being blind to the goodness of God and others.

Trait Verse:
Psalm 95:1-3
"Come, let us sing for joy to the Lord; let us shout aloud to the Rock of our salvation. Let us come before Him with thanksgiving and extol Him with music and song. For the Lord is the great God, the great King above all gods."

Visual Reinforcement:
If possible, invite a computer user to demonstrate the use of a computer Bible program like the one David used on SP 32. Or request a copy of a short print-out from a person or company using the program.

Ideas:
Use parts of the student Celebration Plans from SP 33 to lead your students in worship.

Use as Desired:
SP 33, Giant Think Thanks

PART B: ORDERLINESS

Purpose:
To instruct the students in the steps necessary to plan an event.

Approach:
Orderliness is more than keeping my room clean. There are certain orderly steps that I can take to plan a special event.

Definition:
Putting things and plans in their right places.

Opposite:
Allowing things and plans to become confusing.

Trait Verse:
Esther 4:15-17
"Then Esther sent this reply to Mordecai: 'Go, gather together all the Jews who are in Susa, and fast for me. Do not eat or drink for three days, night or day. I and my maids will fast as you do. When this is done, I will go to the king, even though it is against the law. And if I perish, I perish.'"

Visual Reinforcement:
Display the plans and posters of the special events from SP 35.

Ideas:
Show your students the organization required in putting together your lesson plans.

Organize your students into prayer groups for the duration of the unit. Review concept of faith from Unit Two.

Use as Desired:
SP 34, Orderly Plans for People

PART C: SINCERITY

Purpose:
To present within a story, an example of an insincere promise.

Approach:
When I say or do what I really mean, I am being sincere.
I must be careful of making sincere promises that I may not be able to keep.

Definition:
Meaning what I say and do.

Opposite:
Pretending that I mean what I say and do.

Trait Verse:
Proverbs 25:14
"Like clouds and wind without rain is a man who boasts of gifts he does not give."

Visual Reinforcement:
The trait verse, Proverbs 25:14 lends itself to a variety of visual opportunities: assign students to design a rebus; illustrate the verse as a bulletin board; learn it in sign language.

Ideas:
With your class, list common statements that can be both sincere and insincere, such as "You look nice." Discuss what makes it sincere or insincere.

Use as Desired:
Project Servant, TG 90: Serving Young Children.

MY PLAN FOR THIS UNIT

_____

_____

_____

_____

28 INTRO TO UNIT

- Read through text.
  - ◗ Discuss meanings of "persecute," "bless," and "curse."
  - ◗ Re-emphasize that God knows things we do not; He is asking us to obey without understanding when He says to bless our enemies.
  - ◗ Point out that He provides His power to live His way through His spirit.
- Students begin inking in the page.
  - ◗ Continue discussion by reading the account of Stephen's stoning in Acts 7:54-60.
  - ◗ Compare Stephen's words with those of Jesus on the cross in Luke 23-24.
  - ◗ Note that blessing those who curse you takes supernatural power – one of those "explosions of power" sent by God in our weakness.
  - ◗ Call for examples of showing kindness to those who have done wrong to your students or someone they know.

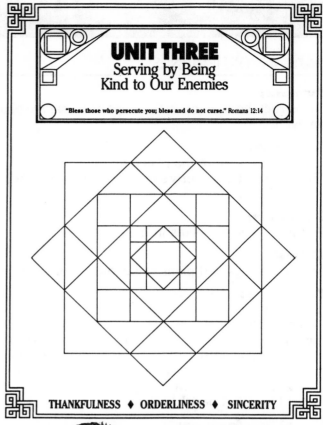

UNIT THREE
Serving by Being
Kind to Our Enemies

"Bless those who persecute you; bless and do not curse." Romans 12:14

THANKFULNESS ♦ ORDERLINESS ♦ SINCERITY

29 ESTHER ILLUSTRATION

- Study and discuss the picture.
  - ◗ Ask: What clues are there in the picture that express the kinds of people Haman and Mordecai are? What emotions would you say are being experienced in this scene?
- Prior to reading the story, discuss the reasons that could have been behind Mordecai's refusal to bow to Haman.

Mordecai refuses to bow to Haman.

EPISODE THREE

BACK FIRE

ESTHER

It took a good long time for the excitement over Queen Esther to subside. When it did, King Xerxes made another announcement that quickly spread through the kingdom.

The announcement said, "Let it be known that Haman, son of Hammedatha, the Agagite, has been promoted to a seat of honor higher than all other leaders. Everyone will bow in honor to him."

Haman loved being important. He bragged about himself to his family and friends and liked giving orders at the palace. When he would walk through the palace gates, the people there would bow to him. He especially loved this part of his job. It gave him even more reason to strut about in a conceited way.

When Haman walked through the gate past Mordecai, however, Mordecai would not bow. At first, Haman did not notice. The guards at the gate tried to convince Mordecai to give honor to Haman, but Mordecai refused. They told Haman that Mordecai was not bowing to him. Haman did not like the news.

The next time Haman passed through the gate, he looked for Mordecai. It was easy to find him, because he was the only one standing. Each time this happened, Haman became more angry and the wickedness of his plan against Mordecai grew more evil.

Haman had found out that Mordecai was a Jew. "I won't kill just Mordecai," thought Haman. "I'll trick the king into killing all of the Jews in Persia! Yes! That's what I'll do."

The first step of the evil trick was choosing a day for the slaughter to take place. It would happen on the thirteenth day of the month of Adar. The next step would be getting permission from the king to carry out the plan. Haman was an expert liar, and his practice of stretching the truth served him as he spoke to the king.

"King Xerxes, there is a certain group of people scattered around your kingdom who keep themselves separate from the rest of us. They have different customs, and they do not obey your laws. It isn't in your best interest to tolerate this." Then Haman added, "I will be glad to add about 10,000 talents of silver to your treasury to help pay the soldiers to destroy these people."

"Keep the money," said the king, "and do with them as you please." King Xerxes removed his ring and gave it to Haman. This meant that he was giving Haman permission to do anything he wanted.

Haman called the palace secretaries together and wrote out the decree in everyone's language. Haman sealed each copy of the degree with the imprint of the king's own ring. This showed that the king approved of the plan. The notice said that on the thirteenth of Adar all Jewish men, women, and children would be killed.

Haman was pleased with himself. The king had fallen for his trick, and soon Mordecai and everyone like him would pay for their mistake. What Haman did not know was that Esther was also a Jew.

30 BACKFIRE: Episode Three Of The Esther Story

- Review past episodes with your class.
- Story
  ◗ Read together or individually.

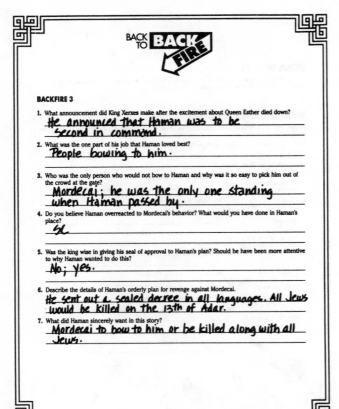

BACK TO BACK FIRE

BACKFIRE 3

1. What announcement did King Xerxes make after the excitement about Queen Esther died down?
   He announced that Haman was to be second in command.

2. What was the one part of his job that Haman loved best?
   People bowing to him.

3. Who was the only person who would not bow to Haman and why was it so easy to pick him out of the crowd at the gate?
   Mordecai; he was the only one standing when Haman passed by.

4. Do you believe Haman overreacted to Mordecai's behavior? What would you have done in Haman's place?
   SL

5. Was the king wise in giving his seal of approval to Haman's plan? Should he have been more attentive to why Haman wanted to do this?
   No; yes.

6. Describe the details of Haman's orderly plan for revenge against Mordecai.
   He sent out a sealed decree in all languages. All Jews would be killed on the 13th of Adar.

7. What did Haman sincerely want in this story?
   Mordecai to bow to him or be killed along with all Jews.

31 BACK TO BACKFIRE

- Complete questions as a group or individually.
  ◗ Discuss answers.
  ◗ Pursue issues that you believe seem most interesting to the students.

32 THANKFULNESS

- Read about David's experiences together.
  - ◗ Discuss as time and interest permit.
- Direct students to locate a verse in Psalms which contains the word "thank" in some form.
  - ◗ Call on students to stand in a circle and read their verses, forming a "Thanks Chain."
- Call on students to offer advice to David and others who have trouble expressing gratitude.
  - ◗ Note that adults who have trouble expressing gratitude are those who did not learn the habit when they were young. Now it is very difficult for them to say "Thanks."

33 THINK THANKS

- Five things
  - ◗ Lead students in thinking of five reasons for thankfulness.
  - ◗ Join them in the activity.
  - ◗ Read, collect, and post the results.
- Director of Celebration
  - ◗ Complete the exercise as directed.
  - ◗ Generate enthusiasm for the freedom we have in celebrating God creatively.
  - ◗ Help them imagine God's joy over watching them think of ways to celebrate His goodness.

 SPIN-OFF

GIANT THINK THANKS. Make a giant compilation of all of the reasons your students are thankful from "Think Thanks." Extend it from floor to ceiling or around the room, writing the words large enough for everyone to read. Enlist the help of your students.

Serve your students by expressing thanks to them.

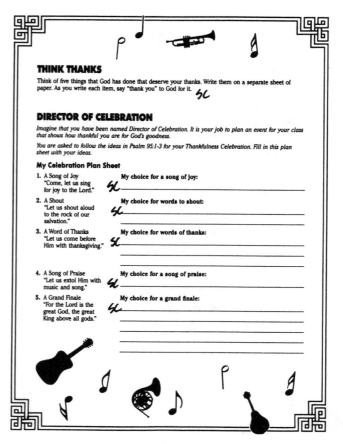

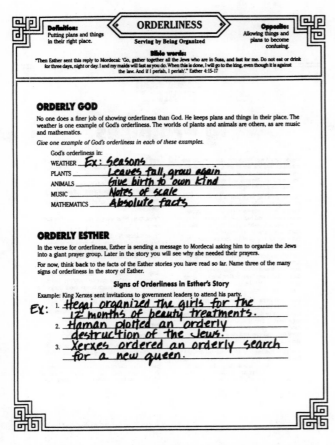

ORDERLINESS
Serving by Being Organized

Definition:
Putting plans and things in their right place.

Opposite:
Allowing things and plans to become confusing.

Bible words:
"Then Esther sent this reply to Mordecai: 'Go, gather together all the Jews who are in Susa, and fast for me. Do not eat or drink for three days, night or day. I and my maids will fast as you do. When this is done, I will go to the king, even though it is against the law. And if I perish, I perish.'" Esther 4:15-17

ORDERLY GOD

No one does a finer job of showing orderliness than God. He keeps plans and things in their place. The weather is one example of God's orderliness. The worlds of plants and animals are others, as are music and mathematics.

Give one example of God's orderliness in each of these examples.

God's orderliness in:

WEATHER __Ex: Seasons__
PLANTS __Leaves fall, grow again__
ANIMALS __Give birth to own kind__
MUSIC __Notes of scale__
MATHEMATICS __Absolute facts__

ORDERLY ESTHER

In the verse for orderliness, Esther is sending a message to Mordecai asking him to organize the Jews into a giant prayer group. Later in the story you will see why she needed their prayers.

For now, think back to the facts of the Esther stories you have read so far. Name three of the many signs of orderliness in the story of Esther.

Signs of Orderliness in Esther's Story

Example: King Xerxes sent invitations to government leaders to attend his party.

EX: 1. __Hegai organized the girls for the 12 months of beauty treatments.__
2. __Haman plotted an orderly destruction of the Jews.__
3. __Xerxes ordered an orderly search for a new queen.__

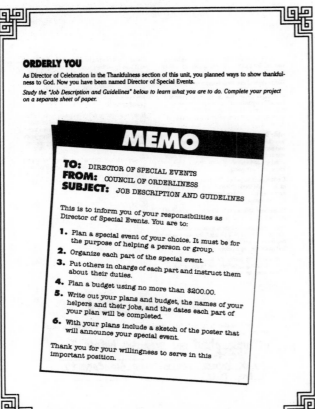

ORDERLY YOU

As Director of Celebration in the Thankfulness section of this unit, you planned ways to show thankfulness to God. Now you have been named Director of Special Events.

Study the "Job Description and Guidelines" below to learn what you are to do. Complete your project on a separate sheet of paper.

MEMO

TO: DIRECTOR OF SPECIAL EVENTS
FROM: COUNCIL OF ORDERLINESS
SUBJECT: JOB DESCRIPTION AND GUIDELINES

This is to inform you of your responsibilities as Director of Special Events. You are to:

1. Plan a special event of your choice. It must be for the purpose of helping a person or group.
2. Organize each part of the special event.
3. Put others in charge of each part and instruct them about their duties.
4. Plan a budget using no more than $200.00.
5. Write out your plans and budget, the names of your helpers and their jobs, and the dates each part of your plan will be completed.
6. With your plans include a sketch of the poster that will announce your special event.

Thank you for your willingness to serve in this important position.

34 ORDERLINESS

- Read trait information together.
  - Quiz briefly.
  - Discuss.
- Orderly God
  - Read text.
  - Compare ideas of God's orderliness.
- Orderly Esther
  - Read text.
  - Instruct students to complete the page.
  - Discuss student responses to orderliness in the Esther story.

■ SPIN-OFF

ORDERLY PLANS FOR PEOPLE. Divide your class into orderly teams. Each team is given one of the following plans of God to analyze: The plan of (1) salvation, (2) marriage, (3) Body of Christ, (4) families, (5) church. Students write out the steps of each plan, or main parts of the plan, and present them to the class.

NOTE: This activity may require more than one session.

---

35 ORDERLY YOU

- Read text and memo together.
- Provide quality time for students to complete this activity.
- Encourage creativity, praising the ideas and efforts of your students.
- Reinforce ideas of delegating and punctuality in reporting.
  - Note the special abilities of students in various areas.
  - Comment and praise.
  - Find ways in the future to let them serve you with those skills.

Serve your students by being an orderly planner.

36 SINCERITY: PROJECT SERVANT STORY AND INTERMISSION

- Story
  - ◆ Instruct students to read the story.
- Intermission
  - ◆ Provide time for students to consider what two rules Darcie could follow to prevent a repeat occurrence.
  - ◆ If time permits, ask students to consider how David, Tony, and Henry might have faced the problem if they had been in Darcie's position.
- Discuss the story, using the following questions as indicators of the degree of retention of the students.

37 STORY, CONTINUED, AND FOLLOW-UP QUESTIONS

- Follow-up questions:
  1. What was the group's fourth project? [Helping young children.]
  2. How did the idea for this project begin? [David went to a children's ward in a hospital to visit his cousin.]
  3. What promise did Darcie make to the children? [The biggest party ever.]
  4. What was keeping Darcie from fulfilling her promise? [Clown out of town; balloon money spent; Mom too busy to make goodies.]
  5. What was Darcie's usual method of dealing with unpleasant thoughts? [Put them out of her mind.]
  6. What was Darcie's greatest fear? [That the children would hate her.]
  7. What did Betty do to help Darcie? [Arranged for Tony to be clown, David to deliver balloons, Henry to draw pictures, she and her mom to bake goodies.]
  8. Although she was fearful about doing so, Darcie did something that took courage. What was it? [Told class she could not keep her promise.]
  9. What struggle might Betty have faced in deciding to help Darcie in this way? ["If I help her, she may just make this mistake again."]
  10. If you had been Darcie, how would you have handled the problem? If you were Betty? [Student choice.]

The Project Servant suggestions for this unit may be found on page 90 of this book.

Definition: Truly meaning what I say and do.

SINCERITY

Opposite: Pretending that I mean what I say and do.

Serving by Being "Real"

Bible words:
"Like clouds and wind without rain is a man who boasts of gifts he does not give." Proverbs 25:14

Big Promises

Darcie meant well when she promised the pre-schoolers that she would bring a clown and presents and lots of food to them on Thursday. But here it was Monday and she had no clown or presents and no sign of special food.

Darcie's plan had been part of the fourth project for the group. Each member was to do something for young children. The idea had come from a visit David had made to his cousin's hospital room when she was having her tonsils out. David wasn't one to get worked up about things, but when he saw all of the children there, he wanted to help them.

He had returned with a video that he and his father had filmed the summer before in their backyard. It was called "The Mystery of the Buried Footprints." His mother had sent along some popcorn for the kids to eat while they watched the video.

Darcie lived near a pre-school. She received permission to be a helper for two weeks as part of the group's project. One day when she was reading a book to the children about parties, she got carried away and promised them the biggest party they had ever had. Now, one week later, she was sorry about the promise.

The party had become an unpleasant thought to Darcie because she had realized that it was not going to work out. Darcie didn't like thinking unpleasant thoughts, so she chose not to think about the party at all. That only worked for one

day, however, and by Tuesday Darcie was upset and tearful. When she and Betty were alone, Darcie told her the ugly story.

"You have to tell the kids that you can't give them the party you promised," advised Betty.

"No, I can't do that!" cried Darcie. "It'll make them sad."

"Well, then, what are you going to do?" asked Betty.

"I don't know. My dad can't be the clown because he's going out of town. I've spent my allowance on other things so I can't buy the balloons. And Mom says she doesn't have time to make anything more than cookies this week for the kids."

Betty listened and comforted her friend. When Darcie left, she was glad for Betty's kindness, but she didn't feel much better about things. Out loud she said, "I hope I'll think about my words before I make any more big promises."

"Darcie! Darcie! Come here!" The children at the pre-school had spotted her. "Only two days until our party."

"Uh, yes. Two days . . ." mumbled Darcie.

The day of the party arrived too soon to suit her. She dreaded showing up with just a little plate of cookies and one big excuse. Darcie may have gotten carried away with her promises, but she was no coward. She would face the kids and tell them the truth. "We'll have our party," she

---

thought. "But it will just be a simple one." She was worried that the children would hate her for it.

Darcie greeted the pre-schoolers with a half-hearted smile. All of them were waiting for her in an eager circle. "Where are the balloons and clown?" they asked. Darcie stepped closer to them to break the bad news. "Well, about the party. It, uh. Well, sometimes things don't . . . I mean . . ."

While Darcie was struggling with her words, Tony was outside struggling with the clown suit he had secretly borrowed from Darcie's father. He was surprised to see David walking to the door with pink and yellow balloons. "Hey, I didn't know you were going to be here," said Tony.

David looked surprised. "Me neither, as a matter of fact," said David. "Betty called me last night and asked if I would deliver some balloons to this pre-school."

"Same here. It looks as if Betty has a project of her own going on here," said Tony.

Betty's voice reached them from the sidewalk. "Go on in. Hurry! We'll be late." She was carrying two boxes of goodies that she and her mother had made the night before.

Tony and David opened the door in time to hear Darcie fumbling for words and finally saying, "There won't be a big party, kids."

"What do you mean, there won't be a big party," said Tony in a clown voice that surprised even him. "I'm here, and where I am there are big parties!"

"Darcie, you were just fooling us!" said Susan, a brown-eyed three-year-old. Darcie was too surprised to speak.

Henry managed to finish his paper route in time to get to the party and draw cartoons for the children. Everyone had a good time, even the clown and balloon man. Darcie took Betty aside and said, "Thank you, Betty, for getting me out of this."

"You're welcome, Darcie," said Betty. "What's the good of helping others all of the time if we can't help each other, too?"

 INTER**MISSION**

Write two rules that Darcie could follow in the future to keep herself from making promises she can't keep.

Ex: 1. <u>Think about my promises before I make them.</u>
2. <u>Ask before committing someone to my plan.</u>

◼ NEXT-TIME NOTES
to make next time better

SP 28: _____

SP 29: _____

SP 30: _____

SP 31: _____

SP 32: _____

SP 33: _____

SP 34: _____

SP 35: _____

SP 36: _____

SP 37: _____

PROJECT SERVANT: _____

OTHER: _____

🌀 AFTERTHOUGHTS
Thoughts too good to lose • Kidquotes • Thoughts from God • Ideas

_____

_____

_____

_____

_____

STEP ONE

Yesterday was November 30. Sometime during the night the air in my classroom turned "Christmas." Though its arrival has been unspoken, everyone in my room knows it is here. It is on their faces, in their steps, and under their skin. The issue is, will I let them get under mine. You know what I mean.

I must make a quick choice. This month will irritate me or delight me. Intrude or inspire. I can say, "I GET to be with children in December, or I HAVE to be with children in December." It is my choice.

By choosing to squeeze the best out of December, I am demonstrating to my students the very qualities I am teaching them.

- They will observe MEEKNESS as I become a member, with them, of the audience of Christmas, thrilling over the drama and intrigue of the true and living God infiltrating the ranks of man in order to change man's destiny.

- They will observe LOYALTY as I stay true to the Christ of Christmas, refusing to "x" Him out of the festivities, exalting Him as the reason for the season's glow. They will watch me be loyal to them as the symptoms of holiday-itis overtake them, causing them to break out in a rash of nonsense.

- They will observe JOY as I delight in being a child of God who is celebrating her Savior's success, rejoicing in His willingness to agree to such a plan on her behalf.

Living out the qualities of meekness, loyalty, and joy is not a December only, Unit Four kind of lifestyle. However, they do look especially lovely right now. Perhaps this is because they were first seen in the life of the One we love.

I really have no choice, after all. Merry Christmas, lovers of children.

PATTERNING

God came down to our level. He brought us to His Father with meekness, loyalty, and love. When we approach our students with meekness, loyalty, and love, then they will more easily understand what God is like. Getting down to their level is God-like and puts stringing popcorn in a heavenly light.

CHEWABLES
Bite-sized thoughts from God's Word

Select a thought to "chew on" during this unit:

"Your attitude should be the same as that of Christ Jesus: Who, being in very nature God, did not consider equality with God something to be grasped, but made Himself nothing, taking the very nature of a servant, being made in human likeness."
Philippians 2:5-7

"In these last days (God) has spoken to us by His Son, whom He appointed heir of all things, and through whom He made the universe."
Hebrews 1:2

"The Son is the radiance of God's glory and the exact representation of His being, sustaining all things by His powerful Word."
Hebrews 1:3

UNIT INFORMATION

Theme Verse:
"Rejoice with those who rejoice." Romans 12:15

Esther Study:
Esther is asked to risk her life for her people.

PART A: MEEKNESS

Purpose:
To present one boy's struggle with pride.

Approach:
I am showing meekness when I share the spotlight with others.

Definition:
Serving others with the abilities God has given me.

Opposite:
Showing off with the abilities God has given me.

Trait Verse:
Romans 12:16
"Live in harmony with one another. Do not be proud, but be willing to associate with people of low position. Do not be conceited."

Visual Reinforcement:
Using the abilities of some of your students, instruct them to make a poster using the unit subtitle and theme verse as its main focus.

Make a collage that pictures people using their abilities. Point out that talent is an extension of God's own creativity coming out in the people He has made.

Ideas:
Attend an event, such as a symphonic performance, with your class. Follow the field trip with a discussion of the willingness of each instrumentalist to team his/her abilities with those of others.

Discover the hidden talents of the students in your class by providing a variety of activities designed to squeeze out student abilities. Plan a day of drama, a needlework project, a musical performance – vocal and instrumental, and a creative writing project with accompanying illustrations. Look for background talent, such as coordinating and directing abilities.

Use as Desired:
TG 91, Project Servant: Serving Senior Citizens

PART B: LOYALTY

Purpose:
To provide examples of loyalty.
To give one example of Jesus' loyalty to God's children.

Approach:
Loyalty is required in every area of my life.
A person can be loyal at any age.
Jesus stays loyal to His followers.

Definition:
Staying true to those I serve.

Opposite:
Staying true to only myself.

Trait Verse:
Esther 8:6
"For how can I bear to see disaster fall on my people? How can I bear to see the destruction of my family?"

Visual Reinforcement:
Loyalty line-up. Recall with your students figures in American history who showed loyalty to their country.

Ideas:
Invite a serviceman in to explain a soldier's view of loyalty. How do soldiers show loyalty? What are they willing to risk and why?

Use as Desired:
SP 41, Loyalty Look-Out

PART C: REVERENCE

Purpose:
To acquaint students with the reverence of those in Heaven for Jesus.
To survey the methods of showing reverence for God on earth – in Bible time and today.

Approach:
God is awesome.
I can show my reverence for Him in many ways.
I will praise Him with all of His other children one day if I am His child.

Definition:
Feeling a deep respect and awe for someone.

Opposite:
Not thinking very highly of a person.

Trait Verse:
Revelation 7:11, 12
"All the angels were standing around the throne and around the elders and the four living creatures. They fell down on their faces before the throne and worshipped God, saying: 'Amen! Praise and glory and wisdom and thanks and honor and power and strength be to our God for ever and ever. Amen!' "

Visual Reinforcement:
Use the pictures from SP 43 spin-off as a bulletin board.

Construct a worship scene by instructing your students to cut out or draw an almost life-size mural of silhouettes praising God. Use the trait verse as a starting point.

Ideas:
Encounters of the God Kind. Conduct a survey with your students of the ways people in the Old Testament (and Saul in the New Testament) responded to encounters with God. List your findings. Let students be awed by the majesty and holiness that surround God.

Use as Desired:
SP 43, Aah'some

MY PLAN FOR THIS UNIT

_____

_____

_____

_____

38 INTRO TO UNIT

- Read through text.
- Discuss rejoicing with one another.
  - As students ink in the page, talk about rejoicing.
  - Read John 2. Jesus is celebrating a wedding.
  - Discuss occasions for rejoicing.
  - Pinpoint specific reasons to rejoice in school: good test scores; election of officers.
  - Spend time discussing the emotions that keep us from wanting to rejoice.
- Circulate as you talk, enjoying students' work and this informal time together.

39 MEEKNESS: PROJECT SERVANT STORY AND INTERMISSION

- Present trait information.
  - Drill and review this and past traits, theme verse.
- Instruct students to read the story.
  - Quiz briefly for general comprehension.
- Intermission
  - Give students time to contemplate their choice for involvement in a Christmas program and their choice of words for letting others know of their desire.
  - Call on students to explain their choices.
  - Keep their responses in mind for future program activities.

UNIT FOUR
Serving by
Sharing Joy

"Rejoice with those who rejoice." Romans 12:15

MEEKNESS ◆ LOYALTY ◆ REVERENCE

Definition: Serving others with the abilities God has given me.

MEEKNESS

Serving by Being Humble

Opposite: Showing off with the abilities God has given me.

Bible words:
"Live in harmony with one another. Do not be proud, but be willing to associate with people of low position. Do not be conceited." Romans 12:16

David's Bout With Conceit

"I'm so excited!" shrieked Darcie. "The people at the senior center will just **love** our program!" The others agreed. The group had enjoyed helping Darcie at the preschool party. Now they wanted to serve the people at the other end of the age ladder.

David was making plans in his head for the solo he hoped to sing. "If I hint around enough, the group will ask me to sing," he thought.

He cleared his throat. "I sang at my church program last spring. Everyone said I did really well." "That's nice," said Betty, turning to Darcie. "How many candy canes are you putting into the Christmas stockings?"

To Henry, David said, "Maybe one of us should sing a Christmas carol alone." "Yeah, maybe," said Henry, watching Jerome. "Jerome, don't get any ideas. This candy is for **people**, not dogs." The dog wagged his tail, hoping that Henry didn't mean it.

David's mouth was open for hint number three when Betty's mother called to him. "David, your mother is here for you." He walked curiously to Betty's front door.

"Hi, David," said his mother. "Dad and I have to go to Grandma's early, so we're picking you up now." David was too logical to argue, so he hollered his goodbyes and headed for the car. All the way to Grandma's, he planned his song.

The next day at school, David found the group and asked about the plans for the program. "Here is a copy of what we decided to do," said Betty.

"Yeah," said Tony, "we knew you would like us to write it out for you. Sorry it's not a print-out." Everyone laughed. David would have laughed, too, if he hadn't just seen the third line of the program. It said: "Solo by Tony." Line eight said, "Lights and mikes handled by David."

David smashed his paper into a ball and threw it into the nearest garbage can. The group watched in shock as he stomped off chewing on the last of some string cheese. "What is wrong with **him**?" asked Tony.

What was wrong was that David was upset because none of his hints worked. "They'll be sorry

44

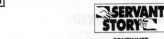
CONTINUED

that I'm not singing instead of him," thought David.

Rehearsals began the next day. David showed up to work the lights and the mikes, but his proud heart was bitter. Betty practiced her cello solo, Darcie told her Christmas story, Henry worked on painting the background scene, and Tony practiced his song. They each tried to talk to David, but he would not talk back to them. No amount of logic could seep through his anger.

After the third practice, Tony caught up with David on his bike. "David, I want to tell you something." David didn't answer. "I want to tell you that I'm sorry you're upset. I'd like to fix whatever is wrong, but I can't do it if I don't know what it is."

"Okay. I'll tell you what is wrong," said David, stopping on the side of the road. "I am a better singer than you are, yet you are the one singing at the Christmas program. I hinted all around that I wanted to do it, but you guys didn't pay any attention to me."

Tony looked surprised. "I didn't know you wanted to sing. I'm sorry." David got back on his bike and headed home at top speed. Tony caught up with him again.

"David," he said, panting, "you're being unreasonable. You're always telling us to think things through, to be logical. Well, take your own ad-

vice. You're being conceited and proud and unforgiving." David jerked his head around to look at Tony. "It is not logical to expect people to catch your hints, David. If you want to do something, isn't it **logical** to come right out and say it?"

Tony rode off, leaving David to think about his words. By the next morning, David had worked out his problem. His father had helped him give up his anger and conceit by talking it over between themselves and God. He apologized to the group.

During Tony's song at that day's practice, David was working the mikes and humming along. "That sounds great," said Darcie. "You were harmonizing without even thinking about it!"

Henry overheard Darcie's comment and said, "Maybe David and Tony should sing a duet." The others agreed.

"How do you feel about that, Tony?" asked David.

"Let's try it," he said with a grin. It worked, and the solo became a duet. "I guess I should use my voice for singing, not bragging," said David.

"I won't argue with that logic," laughed Tony.

INTER**MISSION**

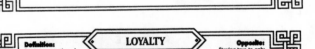

Imagine that you are at a planning meeting for a Christmas program. What activity would you most want to do? *SC* _____

Keeping meekness in mind, plan a set of words that you could use to let the others know what you want to do. *SC* _____

Definition:
Staying true to those I serve.

LOYALTY
Serving by Being Faithful

Opposite:
Staying true to only myself.

Bible Words:
"For how can I bear to see disaster fall on my people? How can I bear to see the destruction of my family?" Esther 8:6

"Not My Brother!"

Two of Henry's older brothers, Robbie and Matt, were at the grocery store on an errand for their mother. While they were choosing a sack of potatoes, a scowling woman came up to them. "That brother of yours!" she cried. "He's lying to me. He says he has delivered my papers this week, but he hasn't!"

Robbie dropped the sack of potatoes back into the bin and turned to face the angry woman. Before he had a chance to speak, Matt said, "If Henry said he delivered your papers, then he did."

"That's right," added Robbie, "Our brother doesn't lie!"

"Well, he sure did lie to me!" she said.

"Me, too," said another woman nearby. "It's been three days since I've gotten my morning paper."

"Well, something must be happening to them after they are delivered, because our brother would not lie," said Robbie, leaving the potatoes and heading for the door. Matt picked them up and quickly paid for them. After a few minutes, he caught up with Robbie.

"What do you think, Robbie?" asked Matt.

"I don't know, but we're going to find out." The two boys hurried home to find Henry.

What do you think was causing the papers to disappear? Be ready to talk about your idea.
SC

FAMILY LOYALTY

When Queen Esther saw her people in danger, her loyalty caused her to risk her life for them. This kind of loyalty is one of the beautiful parts of being in a family.

Here is a list of other ways people have shown loyalty to someone in their family. *As you read through the list, imagine how it would feel to receive such loyalty.*

   A sister donated a kidney to her brother.
   A mother stayed up all night with her sick baby.
   A father offered to go to prison for his son.
   A brother gave blood to help his grandfather.

What acts of loyalty do you know about? *SC* _____

---

40 STORY, CONTINUED, AND FOLLOW-UP QUESTIONS

● Follow-up questions:
1. What was David hoping to do at the Christmas party for senior citizens? [Sing a solo.]
2. How did he go about letting the others know what he wanted to do? [Hinted.]
3. Who was given the solo instead of David? [Tony.]
4. What responsibilities were the others given, including David? [Betty, cello solo; Darcie, Christmas story; Henry, painted backgrounds; David, lights and sound.]
5. David became upset when he found out about Tony's solo. In your opinion, how could David have prevented the situation from turning out this way? [Student choice. Suggestion: He could have told the group that he was hoping to sing a solo, instead of relying on hints to do the job.]
6. What is your opinion of Tony's behavior toward David? [Student choice, however, aim to help students see the value of honest confrontation. Consider together how relationships would have been hindered if no one would have approached David and confronted his unreasonableness.]
7. How did David resolve his anger? [Talked it over with his father and God.]
8. What ending did the story have? [Tony and David sang a duet.] Is there another ending you would have preferred? [Student choice.]

41 LOYALTY

● Read and repeat information about loyalty.
● Review past traits.
● "Not My Brother!"
   ◗ Call on students to read the story.
   ◗ Talk about possible reasons the newspapers are disappearing. Suggestions: A dog was taking them; a boy or girl upset with Henry was hiding them.
   ◗ Consider the choices the brothers had; what if they had chosen to be disloyal?
   ◗ What risk did they take by being loyal?
   ◗ Does loyalty depend on the integrity of the one receiving loyalty?
● Family Loyalty
   ◗ Discuss the acts of family loyalty.
   ◗ Collect examples from your students.
   ◗ Be on the look-out for similar examples in the media and follow them carefully with your students.

 **SPIN-OFF**

LOYALTY LOOK-OUT. Launch a loyalty look-out by instructing your students to look for loyalty at home and in the neighborhood. Instruct them to write their observations in a central place, such as a bulletin board or clipboard. Read and discuss.

42 THE LOYAL JESUS

- Read opening text.
- Jesus Remained Loyal.
  - Look up verses.
  - Discuss situations.
  - Help students imagine being in the same situation. Imagine the fear of the disciples and Peter.
  - Discuss whether or not students are prepared to be loyal even when they are afraid.
- Your opinion
  - Read and solicit thoughts on the abuse of grace.
  - References to help: Romans 6:1 and I John 5:2, 3.

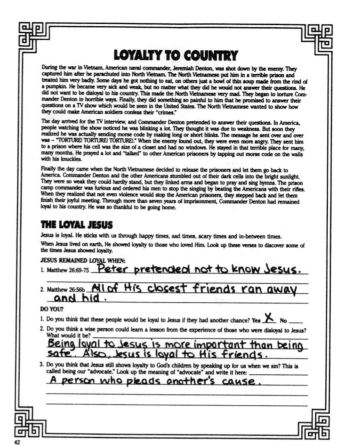

LOYALTY TO COUNTRY

During the war in Vietnam, American naval commander, Jeremiah Denton, was shot down by the enemy. They captured him after he parachuted into North Vietnam. The North Vietnamese put him in a terrible prison and treated him very badly. Some days he got nothing to eat, on others just a bowl of thin soup made from the rind of a pumpkin. He became very sick and weak, but no matter what they did he would not answer their questions. He did not want to be disloyal to his country. This made the North Vietnamese very mad. They began to torture Commander Denton in horrible ways. Finally, they did something so painful to him that he promised to answer their questions on a TV show which would be seen in the United States. The North Vietnamese wanted to show how they could make American soldiers confess their "crimes."

The day arrived for the TV interview, and Commander Denton pretended to answer their questions. In America, people watching the show noticed he was blinking a lot. They thought it was due to weakness. But soon they realized he was actually sending morse code by making long or short blinks. The message he sent over and over was – "TORTURE! TORTURE! TORTURE!" When the enemy found out, they were even more angry. They sent him to a prison where his cell was the size of a closet and had no windows. He stayed in that terrible place for many, many months. He prayed a lot and "talked" to other American prisoners by tapping out morse code on the walls with his knuckles.

Finally the day came when the North Vietnamese decided to release the prisoners and let them go back to America. Commander Denton and the other Americans stumbled out of their dark cells into the bright sunlight. They were so weak they could hardly stand, but they linked arms and began to pray and sing hymns. The prison camp commander was furious and ordered his men to stop the singing by beating the Americans with their rifles. When they realized that not even violence would stop the American prisoners, they stepped back and let them finish their joyful meeting. Through more than seven years of imprisonment, Commander Denton had remained loyal to his country. He was so thankful to be going home.

THE LOYAL JESUS

Jesus is loyal. He sticks with us through happy times, sad times, scary times and in-between times.

When Jesus lived on earth, He showed loyalty to those who loved Him. Look up these verses to discover some of the times Jesus showed loyalty.

JESUS REMAINED LOYAL WHEN:

1. Matthew 26:69-75 ___Peter pretended not to know Jesus.___

2. Matthew 26:56b ___All of His closest friends ran away and hid.___

DO YOU?

1. Do you think that these people would be loyal to Jesus if they had another chance? Yes **X** No ___
2. Do you think a wise person could learn a lesson from the experience of those who were disloyal to Jesus? What would it be? ___
   ___Being loyal to Jesus is more important than being safe. Also, Jesus is loyal to His friends.___
3. Do you think that Jesus still shows loyalty to God's children by speaking up for us when we sin? This is called being our "advocate." Look up the meaning of "advocate" and write it here: ___
   ___A person who pleads another's cause.___

43 REVERENCE

- Read trait information.
  - Review past trait information.
  - Ask various students to say the theme verse.
- Complete page as directed, generating an enthusiasm for showing reverence to a deserving God.

 **SPIN-OFF**

AAH'SOME. Using an entry from the list of #2, students illustrate or cut out examples from a magazine that show a sight or event that awes them. Use on a bulletin board or make into a large book for younger children, perhaps as part of this month's Project Servant.

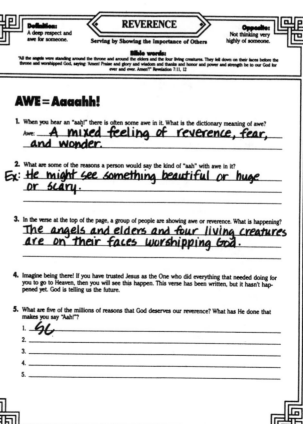

Definition: A deep respect and awe for someone.	REVERENCE Serving by Showing the Importance of Others	Opposite: Not thinking very highly of someone.

Bible words:
"All the angels were standing around the throne and around the elders and the four living creatures. They fell down on their faces before the throne and worshipped God, saying: 'Amen! Praise and glory and wisdom and thanks and honor and power and strength be to our God for ever and ever. Amen!'" Revelation 7:11, 12

AWE = Aaaahh!

1. When you hear an "aah!" there is often some awe in it. What is the dictionary meaning of awe?
   Awe: ___A mixed feeling of reverence, fear, and wonder.___

2. What are some of the reasons a person would say the kind of "aah" with awe in it?
   Ex: ___He might see something beautiful or huge or scary.___

3. In the verse at the top of the page, a group of people are showing awe or reverence. What is happening?
   ___The angels and elders and four living creatures are on their faces worshipping God.___

4. Imagine being there! If you have trusted Jesus as the One who did everything that needed doing for you to go to Heaven, then you will see this happen. This verse has been written, but it hasn't happened yet. God is telling us the future.

5. What are five of the millions of reasons that God deserves our reverence? What has He done that makes you say "Aah!"?
   1. ___sc___
   2. ___
   3. ___
   4. ___
   5. ___

6. We often say "Aah!" about the skills and thrills of athletes, singers, and actors. What has a famous person you admire done to cause you to say "Aah!"?

1. _SL_

2. _SL_

3. _____

4. _____

5. _____

7. What are some ways people show that they think a famous person is awesome?

Ex: clap, cheer, make banners, put them in a parade, make a poster of their picture, write a book about them.

8. Compare your lists in questions 5 and 6.
Which list shows the greatest skills?   #5 ____ #6 ____
Which list deserves the biggest "Aah!"?   #5 ____ #6 ____ *SL*
Which list usually receives the biggest "Aah!"? #5 ____ #6 ____

9. Imagine that everyone who has ever lived and loved God is in one place shouting and singing praises to Him. Imagine that everyone who ever denied that God is real is falling in reverence in front of Him. If you have to choose which group to be in, which group would be your choice? Group 1 or Group 2. That is a choice each person must make.

10. In what ways do people show reverence for God today?
  • In Betty's church, reverence is shown for God by walking and talking quietly and singing songs with organ music about God's greatness.
  • In Tony's church, reverence for God is shown by lively singing and clapping and excited "Amens."
  • In your church, reverence for God is shown by _SL_

11. In what way would you like to show God your reverence, or awe, for Him if He appeared to you today? _SL_

Have you ever thought that He might be pleased if you worshipped Him in this way when you are alone? Many people do.

**GOD IS AWESOME
AND
AAH!SOME!**

44

Esther considers the note that Mordecai sent her about Haman's plan.

44 CONTINUED

● Complete page as directed.
 ◗ Focus on the importance of showing reverence and awe for God in ways that are enjoyable to the individual. From there, point out that this is one reason there are different churches. People worship in different ways.

45 ESTHER ILLUSTRATION

● Study the picture.
 ◗ Ask the class to suggest thoughts which Esther may have been having as she read the note from Mordecai.
 ◗ Ask: What in Esther's expression causes you to know she is contemplating a difficult decision?

46 BACKFIRE: Episode Four Of The Esther Story

- Review past episodes of the story with your class.
- Story
  - Read together or individually.

EPISODE FOUR
BACK FIRE

ESTHER

News of Haman's wicked plan reached Mordecai. His body shook with sorrow and his soul was overcome with heaviness. "My people are facing death for something that I have done," he cried. Weeping bitterly, Mordecai exchanged his everyday clothes for those made of sackcloth, a scratchy piece of clothing reserved for times of mourning. He poured ashes on his head, which showed everyone the extent of his sorrow. Jews everywhere did similar things to show their own distress.

Mordecai, still dressed in sackcloth and wearing ashes, walked through the town to the palace gate. "I must get in touch with Esther," he thought. No one wearing mourning clothes could enter the palace, so he waited there, believing that Esther would hear about him. When Esther's servants saw her cousin, they told her about his condition. "Take these clothes to him!" she said. "He has no reason to do such a thing!" Esther's ears had not yet heard the terrible news.

Mordecai refused to change clothes. Esther knew then that something must have happened. She sent a servant with another message: "What is going on? Why are you mourning?"

Mordecai told the servant everything, even that Haman had wanted to pay the soldiers himself. He gave the servant a copy of the king's decree to give to Esther.

However, Mordecai had more than the news and the decree to give to his cousin, the queen. He had a challenge for her. "Tell Esther to beg the king for mercy and plead with him for her people," he cried. Mordecai was counting on Esther's courage and loyalty to her people to save them.

In the palace, Esther was not feeling courageous. "Go, tell my cousin that everyone here knows that no one just walks in to see the king! I could die if he is not in the mood to see me," she said fearfully.

The servant again met with the wailing Mordecai and spoke Esther's words to him. Through his sorrow, Mordecai said, "Tell the queen these words: Don't think that because you are the queen that your life will be spared. Somehow our people will be delivered; if not by you, then by someone else. But be sure of this, you and I and our family will surely die." Then Mordecai added, "Besides, who is to say that you were not made queen for this very reason?" The servant had written Mordecai's message and quickly took it to the waiting and worried queen.

Esther read the note from her cousin. She had an important choice to make. If she approached the king at the wrong time, she would die. If she didn't approach the king and beg for mercy for her people, she would die anyway. Either way, Esther knew that her life was in danger.

Once again, she sent a message to Mordecai. Mordecai read her note, which said: "Gather our people together and fast for me. Do not eat or drink for three days, night or day. My maids and I will do the same. When the three days are up, I will go into the king even though it is against the law. And, if I die, I die."

Esther had made a choice. Perhaps God did cause her to become queen in order to save His people from death. She chose to show faith. She would serve God and her people with loyalty and courage.

47 BACK TO BACKFIRE

- Complete questions.
  - Discuss answers.
  - Pursue issues that you believe seem most interesting and important to the students.

BACK TO BACK FIRE

BACKFIRE 4

1. What did Mordecai do when he found out about Haman's plan?
   Put on sackcloth and ashes.

2. What was Esther's first reaction to finding out about Mordecai's pitiful condition?
   She wanted him to stop.

3. Why do you think Esther sent a servant to question her cousin? Why didn't she go herself?
   SC

4. What was Mordecai's challenge for Esther? Do you think he ever questioned her loyalty to her people?
   Ask the King for help; SC

5. List Esther's arguments for and against what Mordecai wanted her to do. Pretend that you are her most trusted advisor. Write down some of the things you would say to her.
   SC

6. Find out what it means to be on the "horns of a dilemma." How was Esther in that condition?
   Either way, she was in danger of hurting herself.

7. Look for any examples of meekness, loyalty, and reverence in the story. Share them with a friend.

The Project Servant suggestions for this unit may be found on page 91 of this book.

NEXT-TIME NOTES
to make next time better

SP 38:

SP 39:

SP 40:

SP 41:

SP 42:

SP 43:

SP 44:

SP 45:

SP 46:

SP 47:

PROJECT SERVANT:

OTHER:

AFTERTHOUGHTS
Thoughts too good to lose • Kidquotes • Thoughts from God • Ideas

▶ STEP ONE

Every time I lie I am giving a point to the enemy. I am slam-dunking the ball into the opponent's basket and giving the coach of lies a reason to grin. I don't know about you, but that makes me want to watch what I say and insinuate.

Words. Motives. Actions. So many opportunities for deceit.

"I know I said we could finish the art project today, but we took too long to finish math."

"But teacher, you said I'd get to pass out the papers today." "I meant that some of you would get to do it soon."

"The progress report you sent home said Joe was doing fine, so why did you give him this 'F' "?

"I thought you said your lesson plans were finished." "Well, they nearly were, and then I was interrupted. The weekend was so full that I just didn't get back to them."

For every opportunity to lie, however, there is an equal opportunity to tell the truth. Living truthfully requires self-control and a commitment to please God more than others or myself. It means being sure I am scoring for the right team.

God hates lying. I must let this sink in. Selah.

If God hates a lie
I wonder why I
Who say that I love Him would let one slip by?

It seems such a waste
To let my lips taste
The flavor of something the God I love hates.

PATTERNING

God only speaks the truth. What do you speak? Look over the examples in "Step One" and decide how each situation could have been handled honestly.

Now evaluate the words of your day so far. Have they been honest? Consider the impact an honest teacher can have on students who live in a dishonest world. Finally, consider the importance of speaking honestly about God.

CHEWABLES
Bite-sized thoughts from God's Word

Select one thought to "chew on" during this unit:

"I am angry with you and your two friends, because you have not spoken of me what is right, as my servant Job has."
Job 42:7

"The heart of the righteous weighs its answers, but the mouth of the wicked gushes evil."
Proverbs 15:28

"Keep me from deceitful ways; be gracious to me through Your law. I have chosen the way of truth; I have set my heart on Your laws."
Psalm 119:29, 30

UNIT INFORMATION

Theme Verse:
"Mourn with those who mourn." Romans 12:15

Esther Study:
Esther risks her life by approaching the king with her request.

PART A: SELF-CONTROL

Purpose:
To furnish the student with a plan of self-control. To provide examples of self-control in Bible and everyday situations.

Approach:
Choosing my words carefully will be a help in my life. There are four questions I can ask myself before I speak that will help me control my words.

Definition:
Guarding my life by making right choices.

Opposite:
Letting anything into my life.

Trait Verse:
Proverbs 17:27
"A man of knowledge uses words with restraint, and a man of understanding is even-tempered."

Visual Reinforcements:
Write out and post the Control Check-Point System presented on SP 49.

Ask for volunteers to illustrate the unit's subtitle (Serving by sharing sorrow) and theme verse. Display in your classroom.

Ideas:
To promote the definition of self-control (see above), ask students to compile a list of common choices facing them at home, school, and with friends. Use each entry as a discussion starter during the unit.

Instruct teams of students to modernize the four Bible examples from SP 50 by altering the speech and risks involved. Present them to the class or use as a chapel presentation.

Use as Desired:
SP 48, Mourning Together
SP 49, Check-Points

PART B: HONESTY

Purpose:
To provide the students with an example of honesty in story form.

Approach:
There are times when being honest will frighten me. Being honest with another person is one way I can show God that I trust Him.

Definition:
Being free of lies.

Opposite:
Being full of lies.

Trait Verse:
Proverbs 16:13
"Kings take pleasure in honest lips; they value a man who speaks the truth."

Visual Reinforcement:
Enlarge the "Honesty Workout" title on TG 92 to promote the activity. Place it in the middle of a bulletin board. Surround it with paragraphs written by your students of ways to serve various leaders with honesty.

Ideas:
Using the letters in the word "Honesty," invite your students to team up with a friend to create an acrostic about being truthful.

Invite an employer in to speak to your class about the value of being an honest employee. Prior to the visit, you may wish to have students write questions for the guest to answer.

Use as Desired:
SP 51, Honesties
TG 92, Project Servant: Honesty Workout

PART C: CAUTIOUSNESS

Purpose:
To examine God's cautions about certain types of people.
To stimulate the students' thinking toward choices of friends.

Approach:
God cautions me about avoiding certain kinds of people.
My parents and other leaders also caution me about certain people.
I must learn to discern the kinds of people who will make the best friends for me.

Definition:
Living my life carefully.

Opposite:
Not caring how I live my life.

Trait Verse:
Proverbs 12:26
"A righteous man is cautious in friendship, but the way of the wicked leads them astray."

Visual Reinforcement:
Ask a student to cut out a large caution sign. Mount on bulletin board. Ask students to write out cautions to people in "Backfire!" and this unit's Project Servant stories. Cautions may be written on red circles, representing warning lights, and placed around the caution sign.

Ideas:
With your students, study examples of good and bad influences of one person on another by searching through newspapers and magazines. Discuss and determine the part caution did or did not play in the situation. Example: A drunken driver who wrecks the car and injures passengers.

Use as Desired:
SP 54, Friendly Guidelines

MY PLAN FOR THIS UNIT

_____

_____

_____

_____

48 INTRO TO UNIT

- Read through text.
  - ◆ Define "mourn."
- Ink in the page.
  - ◆ Discuss the subject of mourning as students ink in the page.
  - ◆ If desired, suggest that they use colors that to them symbolize mourning.
  - ◆ Invite students to ask questions about mourning and grief or share personal experiences.
  - ◆ Present these examples of "mourning with those who mourn" as they complete the page.

  1. John 11:33-35. This account of Jesus weeping at the tomb of Lazarus demonstrates His capacity for "mourning with those who mourn." Suggest to your students that the reasons for Christ's tears may have gone beyond the death of Lazarus. Challenge them to give you other reasons that Jesus might have cried at this time. Possible answers: for the ruin sin brought to God's original plan of eternal life; for the lack of faith in Him of the people on earth.

  2. Luke 7:12-15. Jesus is moved with compassion toward a mother at her son's funeral.

  3. Matthew 9:18-26. You may use this account as a discussion-starter about the various ways societies mourn their dead.

■ SPIN-OFF

MOURNING TOGETHER. Use this page as a lead-in to a brief study or discussion about specific ways to mourn with another person. Invite a sensitive counselor to be a guest in your class to answer questions and offer suggestions in the art of sharing grief honestly. Keep the activity practical by providing students with role-playing exercises.

---

49 SELF-CONTROL

- Read and discuss trait information.
  - ◆ Lead the class in a lively drill of past traits and verses.
- Control Check-Points
  - ◆ Re-read verse.
  - ◆ Discuss meanings of "restraint" and "even tempered." Quiz for understanding.
  - ◆ Challenge students to find examples of even-temperedness and controlled speech in adults around them. If desired, ask them to name the people in their lives who seem to be self-controlled in their speech.
  - ◆ Complete remainder of the page. Compare answers and discuss, encouraging students to offer their opinions even if they differ from others in the class.

UNIT FIVE
Serving by
Sharing Sorrow

"Mourn with those who mourn." Romans 12:15

SELF-CONTROL ◆ HONESTY ◆ CAUTIOUSNESS

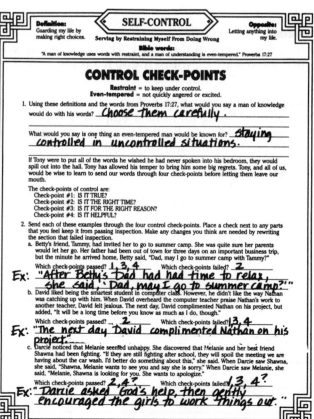

Definition: Guarding my life by making right choices.

◄ **SELF-CONTROL** ►
Serving by Restraining Myself From Doing Wrong

Opposite: Letting anything into my life.

Bible words:
"A man of knowledge uses words with restraint, and a man of understanding is even-tempered." Proverbs 17:27

CONTROL CHECK-POINTS

Restraint = to keep under control.
Even-tempered = not quickly angered or excited.

1. Using these definitions and the words from Proverbs 17:27, what would you say a man of knowledge would do with his words? **Choose them carefully.**

   What would you say is one thing an even-tempered man would be known for? **Staying controlled in uncontrolled situations.**

   If Tony were to put all of the words he wished he had never spoken into his bedroom, they would spill out into the hall. Tony has allowed his temper to bring him some big regrets. Tony, and all of us, would be wise to learn to send our words through four check-points before letting them leave our mouth.

   The check-points of control are:
   Check-point #1: IS IT TRUE?
   Check-point #2: IS IT THE RIGHT TIME?
   Check-point #3: IS IT FOR THE RIGHT REASON?
   Check-point #4: IS IT HELPFUL?

2. Send each of these examples through the four control check-points. Place a check next to any parts that you feel keep it from passing inspection. Make any changes you think are needed by rewriting the section that failed inspection.

   a. Betty's friend, Tammy, had invited her to go to summer camp. She was quite sure her parents would let her go. Her father had been out of town for three days on an important business trip, but the minute he arrived home, Betty said, "Dad, may I go to summer camp with Tammy?"
   Which check-points passed? **1, 3, 4** Which check-points failed? **2**
   Ex: **"After Betty's Dad had had time to relax, she said, 'Dad, may I go to summer camp?'"**

   b. David liked being the smartest student in computer class. However, he didn't like the way Nathan was catching up with him. When David overheard the computer teacher praise Nathan's work to another teacher, David felt jealous. The next day, David complimented Nathan on his project, but added, "It will be a long time before you know as much as I do, though."
   Which check-points passed? **2** Which check-points failed? **3, 4**
   Ex: **"The next day David complimented Nathan on his project."**

   c. Darcie noticed that Melanie seemed unhappy. She discovered that Melanie and her best friend Shawna had been fighting. "If they are still fighting after school, they will spoil the meeting we are having about the car wash. I'd better do something about this," she said. When Darcie saw Shawna, she said, "Shawna, Melanie wants to see you and say she is sorry." When Darcie saw Melanie, she said, "Melanie, Shawna is looking for you. She wants to apologize."
   Which check-points passed? **2, 4?** Which check-points failed? **1, 3, 4?**
   Ex: **"Darcie asked God's help, then gently encouraged the girls to work things out."**

SELF-CONTROL SCAN

1. Search your memory for examples of self-control in the Project Servant stories you have read. Write the examples on these lines: _SC_ _____

2. Scan the Esther stories. Where is the self-control, and who is showing it? _SC_ _____

3. Look back over the last three days. Where and when have you seen children or adults stopping themselves before they did wrong? _SC_ _____

4. Using your memory again, recall these popular Bible stories. Write at least one place in each story where self-control was used or where it was lost.
   a. Samson _Lost control of his words with Delilah_
   b. Annanias and Sapphira _Lost control and lied._
   c. Daniel and the three Hebrew boys _Kept control and remained loyal_
   d. Joseph and Potiphar's wife _Kept control and left the temptation behind._

5. Now run each of these Bible stories through the control check-points. As a story passes a check-mark, place a "+" on the line. As a story fails a check-point, place a "-" on the line. Be ready to suggest ways the failed check-points could be improved with self-control.

STORY	CHECK-POINTS			
a. Samson	#1: +	#2: —	#3: —	#4: —
b. Annanias and Sapphira	#1: +	#2: —	#3: —	#4: —
c. Daniel and the three Hebrew boys	#1: +	#2: +	#3: +	#4: +
d. Joseph and Potiphar's wife	#1: +	#2: +	#3: +	#4: +

6. There are many people serving one another with self-control in your city every day. Right now someone is turning in a wallet of money, choosing not to hit someone, telling the truth instead of a lie, or refusing to eat or drink something that would be harmful.

7. How have you served someone recently by being self-controlled? _SC_ _____

Definition: Being free of lies.	HONESTY	Opposite: Being full of lies.

Serving by Being Truthful
Bible words:
"Kings take pleasure in honest lips; they value a man who speaks the truth." Proverbs 16:13

Milk Money Mess-Up

"Darcie, guess what!" shouted Betty. "Mrs. Stoner is going to take the cook's place for a week while she visits her sick mother. Mrs. Stoner has asked us to collect the milk money in her place."

"Oh, good. I **love** handling money," said Darcie. "I'll go tell the others about it."

Mrs. Stoner collected milk money every morning before school began. She would take the thirty cents for a carton of milk, then give each student a milk ticket. The student would give the ticket to the lunchroom clerk and receive a half-pint of milk.

Betty was the first of the group to collect the milk money. She felt pleased with herself as she put each piece of change into the correct section of the money box. "This is easy," she thought.

Things got more difficult when Peter arrived at the ticket table. "Betty," he said with a smirk, "I forgot my milk money today, but I'll bring it tomorrow. Okay?" She stared at him nervously. "Mrs. Stoner lets me do it all the time," he added.

Relieved to hear the loan was nothing new, Betty said, "Well, if Mrs. Stoner does it, then I guess it would be all right." She gave Peter a milk ticket without having any of his money to put in the money box. By the end of her turn, Betty had granted similar favors to four of Peter's friends.

"I hope no one counts the money until Peter and his friends pay back their loans," thought Betty as she walked to the office with the money

box. In spite of what Peter said, Betty was sure he had lied about Mrs. Stoner and the loans. The secretary was on her way out of the office as Betty put the money on the countertop. "Thanks, Betty. Just leave it on my desk. I will count it when I get back."

Fear grabbed Betty's throat. "Maybe I can find five extra tickets in her desk. I could add five more to the box. Miss Montgomery would think that I had sold five tickets less than I really did." As Betty was opening the drawers, the principal walked in.

"Hello, Betty. What are you doing?" he asked.

"Uh, I'm looking for a stapler," she answered.

"The stapler is right here," he said, pointing to the counter.

"Oh, yes. I looked right past it. Thanks," said Betty with a quiver in her voice. She closed the desk drawers and walked toward the stapler. She fumbled for some papers in her backpack. They didn't really need stapling, but she stapled them anyway.

"I'll be right back," said Mr. Simons. "You'd better be getting to class."

"I will, Mr. Simons. Thanks," she said. Then to herself, she thought, "I've got to get to that box. I'll use my lunch money to make up the difference."

Betty was on her way to Miss Montgomery's desk

 SPIN-OFF

CHECK-POINTS. Using the Control Check-Point system from SP 49, instruct students to analyze hypothetical or real-life situations common today.

50 SELF-CONTROL SCAN

- Complete page as indicated.
  1-3. Search for examples of self-control together, calling on students to name their sightings.
  4-5. Call on students to recall the facts of each story. Adjust the activity to the level and ability of your class.
  6-7. If possible, bring clippings of recent acts of self-control to read to the class.
- Emphasize the idea of serving others by being self-controlled. Consider the many ways we serve one another with self-control. Examples: refusing to spill out our angry thoughts; leaving a stick of gum for the next person; throwing the baseball carefully.

Serve your students by guarding your words.

51 HONESTY: SERVANT STORY AND INTERMISSION

- Present trait information.
- Review past traits and verses.
- Read and discuss story.

 SPIN-OFF

HONESTIES. Provide planned exercises in honesty during the unit. Make arrangements for students to collect milk or lunch money, deliver notes, correct quizzes. Note the honesties you see, giving honest praise in response.

Serve your students by being truthful.

52 STORY, CONTINUED, AND FOLLOW-UP QUESTIONS

● Follow-up questions:

1. Why was Mrs. Stoner going to work in the kitchen for a week? [The cook had to go visit her sick mother.]

2. What was the normal procedure for collecting milk money? [Take the 30¢, give the student a milk ticket, and the student would give the ticket to the lunch-room clerk and receive the milk.]

3. Describe your impression of Peter and his friends. [Student choice.]

4. What helped Betty believe Peter's lie? [He said Mrs. Stoner had loaned him milk money before.]

5. What made her believe later that Peter had lied to her? [She heard him and his friends laughing about their trick.]

6. What incorrect belief did Betty have about the money in the box? [It would be counted at the end of the week instead of daily.]

7. What attempts did Betty make to cover the evidence before Miss Montgomery could count the money? [Tried to find extra tickets in her desk while pretending to be looking for a stapler; tried to put her own money into the box.]

8. What was her final plan and where did she think of it? [To tell Miss Montgomery the truth; in the broom closet.]

9. What course of action do you feel would be appropriate as penalties for Peter and his friends? [Student choice.]

10. What advice do you feel Betty might have given Darcie when they talked after class? [Student choice.]

53 CAUTIOUSNESS

● Read information about cautiousness.
  ◆ Drill for retention.
  ◆ Review past traits.
  ◆ Call on students to recite the theme verse.
● CAUTION: DANGEROUS PEOPLE AHEAD!
  ◆ Read paragraph.
  ◆ Stress the helpfulness of these cautions.
  ◆ Note that the cautions demonstrate God's interest in the way we live our lives. He wants us to lead satisfying lives.
  ◆ Complete the page by breaking the codes and solving the puzzles.
  ◆ Circulate, offering help and encouragement.
  ◆ Compare answers and discuss reasons caution is needed.
  ◆ Call on a student to read each verse.

SERVANT STORY
CONTINUED

with the money in her hand when Mr. Palmer, the school counselor, walked through. "Hi, Betty," he said cheerfully. "Why aren't you in class?"

"I'm helping Miss Montgomery," she answered, wondering how she got into this mess.

"Oh, that's nice. How are you helping her?" he asked.

"I'm counting milk money for her," she answered, feeling more than a little scared. She was not used to lying and she didn't like what it did to her.

"Oh. Well, go right ahead. I'm just doing a little work of my own here," he said as he thumbed through some files.

Betty opened the lid of the money box. "Why are you opening the money box, Betty," asked Miss Montgomery as she entered the office.

"Uh, well, I thought I would count it for you," she said, clutching her own money tightly.

"That's not necessary. It only takes me a minute to do it," she said.

Betty turned and walked from the office still holding her money. She needed a place to think, so she stepped inside the broom closet, which was as unusual an idea to her as lying had been.

Ideas for solving her problem came and went through Betty's mind. Most of them were ridiculous. Only one idea stuck. She left the broom closet and headed back to the office. Before she had taken ten steps, Betty was stopped by Miss Montgomery.

"Betty, may I talk to you?" she said.

"I know what you are going to say," said Betty.

"The milk money is $1.50 short. I was coming back to tell you."

"Can you explain it to me?" asked the secretary, lowering her head to look into Betty's eyes.

The weight of her lies lifted as Betty told Miss Montgomery about the loans she had given to Peter and his friends. "They told me that Mrs. Stoner did it all of the time, but later I heard them laughing about how they had tricked me," she said, ashamed. "I thought you wouldn't count the money until the end of the week, and by then I figured I could make them pay it back. I was about to put in $1.50 when you came back into the office."

Miss Montgomery could see that Betty felt very badly about the wrong choices she had made. "Lying gets a little tricky, doesn't it," said the secretary kindly. "It's never worth it, you know. But I'm pleased that you were coming back to tell me about it. I know you are usually an honest girl, Betty."

They walked to the office together. There, Betty admitted her lies to Mr. Simons and Mr. Palmer. They forgave her and said that they would work things out with the boys and the missing money.

When she finally got to her classroom, Darcie said, "Wow, I didn't know collecting milk money took so long! Was it fun, Betty?"

Betty looked at Darcie and said, "Fun? It might have been if I had remembered that I was a money collector and not a loan officer!" Darcie looked puzzled. "Tell you later," said Betty as she reached for her math test. "I hope **these** numbers add up right," she thought with a grin.

INTER**MISSION**

Use your knowledge of the other servant team members to imagine what similar things might have happened to them on the day they collected milk money for Mrs. Stoner.

Definition:
Living my life carefully.

CAUTIOUSNESS

Opposite:
Not caring how I live my life.

Serving by Being Aware of Danger and Wrong

Bible words:
"A righteous man is cautious in friendship, but the way of the wicked leads them astray." Proverbs 12:26

Some of God's most helpful words to us are His warnings about the kinds of people to avoid. *Find out who to be cautious of by unscrambling the letters and filling in the correct words on each line. The verse next to each scramble marks the place in the Bible where the warning is given.*

SCRAMBLER

EHT EESSIRAHP THE PHARISEES Matt. 16:12
ETH ETPRUTISTO THE PROSTITUTE Prov. 7:10, 24, 25
ELPPEO THWI DBA SRETEMP PEOPLE WITH BAD TEMPERS Prov. 22:24
EOELPP HOW LTEL SESTRCE PEOPLE WHO TELL SECRETS Prov. 20:19
A HISLOOF NERPSO A FOOLISH PERSON Prov. 14:7
A COMKRE A MOCKER Prov. 22:10

OTHER WARNINGS

1. What kinds of people do your parents and other leaders warn you about? What are their reasons?

KINDS OF PEOPLE TO AVOID	REASON

2. Circle the entries on your chart that you believe would also be on God's list.

3. Place an "x" by those entries that may not be on God's list, but that you believe He would want you to avoid anyway.

4. Are there any unmarked entries on your list? Yes _____ No _____

   What does this tell you? _____

5. Sort out the difference between serving the needs of people and "linking up" with them in friendship.

   Would the same cautions apply to both? Yes _____ No **X** Why? *Serving, or helping, someone for Jesus is not the same as being their close friend or companion.*

6. Jesus spent time with people that the Pharisees called "no goods." What does this tell you about people's opinions of one another?

   They are not always accurate.

7. How can a person know whose opinions to take seriously?

   By noting the way a person follows Jesus and deals with people and life.

8. What help could a verse like Proverbs 13:20 be to someone who is wondering about whom to avoid and befriend?

   It would give them a tip about the result of being friends with the wise and foolish.

   Be ready to tell about one time a person has kept you from doing wrong, and one time a person has helped you do wrong.

Esther entertains the king and Haman.

54 OTHER WARNINGS

- Complete the page together or individually.
- Compare and discuss answers.
- Focus on the difference between "serving" and "friending" people.
  ▶ Issue: Can we minister to, or serve, people on God's caution list? If so, what guidelines are wise for us to follow?
- Discuss student experiences of being helped or led astray by a friend.

SPIN-OFF

FRIENDLY GUIDELINES. Translate the cautious and collective wisdom of your students into a list of guidelines for friendship. Post or photocopy as a reminder and service to your students.

Serve your students by correcting them cautiously.

55 ESTHER ILLUSTRATION

- Study the picture.
  ▶ Discuss the banquet.
  ▶ Imagine the conversation and the thoughts of Esther and her guests.

56 BACKFIRE: Episode Five Of The Esther Story

- Introduce this story by asking students to imagine that an entire nation of people was counting on them to correctly approach a king or president and expose his top aide. Consider the pressure, the emotion, the careful choice of words.
- Read the story individually or together.

EPISODE FIVE

BACK FIRE

ESTHER

Stomachs all over the kingdom were raising a fuss. The Jews and Esther had not eaten anything for three days, but no one really cared. After all, they were fasting over an issue of life and death.

On the third day of the fast, Esther kept her promise to Mordecai and the people. She asked her maids to bring out her finest garments and robes. Since she was going to visit the king without being invited, she would look her best. When the time came, she left her part of the palace and walked to the king's court. Her heart was racing within her. "I will know any moment whether I will live or die," she whispered.

She was fearful because she knew that uninvited guests of the king would be killed unless he raised his golden scepter to them. It had been one month since Xerxes had last called for Esther, and she was not sure if her visit would please him.

As Esther stepped into the inner court, the king looked up. She wait'd, breathlessly, for his response. His face showed pleasure as his hand reached for his scepter. Relieved, but not showing it, the queen stepped forward and touched the tip of the golden sword.

"What is it, Esther," he said, smiling. "What do you want? I'll give you anything up to half of the kingdom."

This is exactly what Esther was hoping he would say. "If it pleases the king," she said, "I would like you and Haman to come to a banquet I have prepared for you."

The king, always ready for a party, sent for Haman, and the two men hurried to Esther's banquet room. The invitation made Haman feel more important than ever before, and he enjoyed every bite and drink of the delicious meal.

After dinner, the king, still curious about the reason behind Esther's visit, said, "Now, Esther. What is it you really want? Remember, I will give you up to half of my kingdom."

Esther spoke her words carefully. "If you view me with favor, and if it pleases you, let the king and Haman come tomorrow to another banquet I will prepare for you. It is then that I will answer your question."

"Very well! We'll be delighted to repeat this wonderful idea," said Xerxes, rubbing his stomach.

Haman held in his screams of joy until he passed through the doors of his own house. He was looking forward to another turn at feeling important. "You'll never guess what happened!" he said to his family and friends. "The queen invited the king and I – just us – to a banquet. I spent all afternoon with them – just us – eating and drinking and talking. Imagine, the king and I and Esther – just us!" He stopped for a quick breath, then continued. "And not only that, but she has invited me **back** for another banquet tomorrow!" Haman's pride was overtaking his mouth and he bragged on and on about himself, his job, his family, and his special friendship with Esther and the king. If Haman had been any more puffed up about himself, he would have been a balloon.

Suddenly, Haman's mind popped his balloon of pride by showing him a picture of Mordecai standing while others bowed to him. "None of these good things really matter to me as long as that Mordecai refuses to honor me!" The memory of Mordecai had caused Haman's joy to fly out the window, leaving him in a cloud of pout.

"Good grief, Haman!" said his wife and friends. "Just build high gallows for the man, get the king's permission to hang Mordecai in the morning, then go to your banquet and have a good time," advised his friends.

"That is a perfectly wonderful idea!" shouted Haman, feeling more cheerful now. "I'll order it done this very minute." Meanwhile, back at the palace, the king was stroking his beard wondering what Esther wanted, and Esther was deep in thought planning the best way to tell him.

57 BACK TO BACKFIRE

- Complete questions.
  - ▸ Lead the class in an enthusiastic review of the story.
  - ▸ Discuss the answers and share opinions.

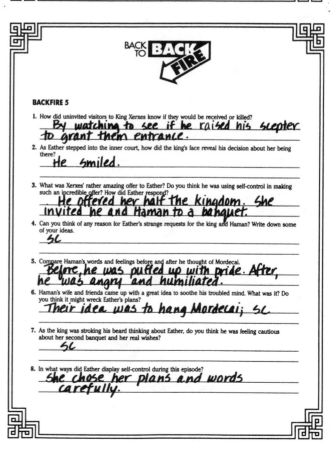

BACK TO BACK FIRE

BACKFIRE 5

1. How did uninvited visitors to King Xerxes know if they would be received or killed?
   By watching to see if he raised his scepter to grant them entrance.

2. As Esther stepped into the inner court, how did the king's face reveal his decision about her being there?
   He smiled.

3. What was Xerxes' rather amazing offer to Esther? Do you think he was using self-control in making such an incredible offer? How did Esther respond?
   He offered her half the kingdom. She invited he and Haman to a banquet.

4. Can you think of any reason for Esther's strange requests for the king and Haman? Write down some of your ideas.
   SC

5. Compare Haman's words and feelings before and after he thought of Mordecai.
   Before, he was puffed up with pride. After, he was angry and humiliated.

6. Haman's wife and friends came up with a great idea to soothe his troubled mind. What was it? Do you think it might wreck Esther's plans?
   Their idea was to hang Mordecai; SC

7. As the king was stroking his beard thinking about Esther, do you think he was feeling cautious about her second banquet and her real wishes?
   SC

8. In what ways did Esther display self-control during this episode?
   She chose her plans and words carefully.

The Project Servant suggestions for this unit may be found on page 92 of this book.

NEXT-TIME NOTES
to make next time better

SP 48:

SP 49:

SP 50:

SP 51:

SP 52:

SP 53:

SP 54:

SP 55:

SP 56:

SP 57:

PROJECT SERVANT:

OTHER:

AFTERTHOUGHTS
Thoughts too good to lose • Kidquotes • Thoughts from God • Ideas

◑ STEP ONE

Eric couldn't face school one day and so he got off the bus, walked into the furnace room and shut the door. There wasn't a teacher in the building who couldn't identify with him. Sometimes school does overwhelm a person.

Eric needed encouragement to persevere. Don't we all.

Perseverance is hard work, an uphill climb that gets toughest just before reaching the peak. Gethsemane proved that. With the finish line around the corner, Jesus wrestled with continuing the climb. However, the joy of looking forward to going home to His Father outdid any urge to quit.

We share that same goal. We are waiting our turn to go home and be with our Father. In the meantime, we are told to look at Jesus to keep from growing weary and losing heart. We are also told to find ways of encouraging one another.

One way is to patiently sit with those who are winded from their diligent climb. Remind them of the goal. There is life beyond the furnace room, but sometimes it looks too steep.

PATTERNING

By completing the job He was sent to do, Jesus left us a clear-cut example of perseverance. If we choose to pattern this quality in our lives, our students will gain a double benefit: they will read about it in the Bible, and they will watch it in us. Judge honestly your own diligence, then study Hebrews 12:1-12 for encouragement in patient perseverance.

CHEWABLES
Bite-sized thoughts from God's Word

Select one of these thoughts to "chew on" during the unit:

"I have brought You glory on earth by completing the work You gave me to do." John 17:4

"Love is patient . . . love always perseveres." I Corinthians 13:4, 7

"Forgetting what is behind and straining toward what is ahead, I press on toward the goal to win the prize for which God has called me heavenward in Christ Jesus. All of us who are mature should take such a view of things." Philippians 3:13-15

UNIT INFORMATION

Theme Verse:
"Live in harmony with one another." Romans 12:16

Esther Study:
Mordecai is led through the streets in honor by an embarrassed Haman.

PART A: DILIGENCE

Purpose:
To acquaint the student with examples of diligent errand running.

To identify common hindrances to diligence.

Approach:
There are many excuses for not being diligent. I can choose to ignore the excuses and be responsible.

Definition:
Doing my work steadily until it is done.

Opposite:
Quitting when I feel like it.

Trait Verse:
Proverbs 25:13
"Like the coolness of snow at harvest time is a trustworthy messenger to those who send him; he refreshes the spirit of his masters."

Visual Reinforcement:
Message Center. Suggest situations that would require important messages to be delivered. Examples: A child has fallen into a ditch and broken her leg; a house is on fire; an unemployed man receives a call for an immediate interview; a lost child is found. Students write appropriate messages for each of the many situation titles you place on a bulletin board titled "Message Center."

Ideas:
Study the details of the situations presented on TG 60 and TG 61. Use the study to raise awareness of other important examples of diligent "message sending" today.

Use as Desired:
SP 60, Famous Messages
SP 62, God's Unseen Hand

PART B: PATIENCE

Purpose:
To offer the student some reasons to look forward to Heaven.

To encourage him/her to wait patiently for Jesus.

To provide examples of things to do to earn treasure in Heaven.

Approach:
Heaven is better than anyone can imagine.

While I wait for Jesus, there are things I can do to prepare myself.

Definition:
Choosing to wait with calmness.

Opposite:
Letting anger rule my waiting.

Trait Verse:
James 5:7, 8
"Be patient, then, brothers, until the Lord's coming. See how the farmer waits for the land to yield its valuable crop and how patient he is for the fall and spring rains. You too, be patient and stand firm, because the Lord's coming is near."

Visual Reinforcement:
Title a bulletin board with "Packing My Bags For Heaven." Students illustrate, label, or cut out pictures of activities and relationships which can result in lasting treasure.

Ideas:
Run a search for patience in the Esther stories presented so far. With your class, determine how the story might have been different at this point had anyone given in to impatience.

Use the idea of investments to serve as an introduction to a unit on the correct use of money. Invite knowledgeable parents or friends to explain basic banking and budgeting strategies to your class. The point: Money used correctly can be useful in building treasure in heaven.

Use as Desired:
SP 64, Ways of Waiting

PART C: THOROUGHNESS

Purpose:
To provide the student with examples of thoroughness.
To offer an exercise in thoroughness.

Approach:
Thoroughness may take longer, but its benefits are worth it.

Definition:
Completing the details of a task.

Opposite:
Overlooking the details of a task.

Trait Verse:
Psalm 138:8
"The Lord will fulfill His purpose for me; Your love, O Lord, endures forever – do not abandon the works of Your hands."

Visual Reinforcement:
Define, illustrate, and explain the reason for "thorough" in words such as "thoroughfare" and "thoroughbreds." Use as a bulletin board or daily update on thoroughness.

Ideas:
Using a map of your city or state, analyze the thoroughness necessary in street and freeway planning. Consider other occupations and their requirement for thoroughness.

Use as Desired:
SP 66, Thoroughness Theories
TG 93, Project Servant: Sending A Message Thoroughly

MY PLAN FOR THIS UNIT

_____

_____

_____

_____

58 INTRO TO UNIT

- Read through text.
- Discuss the meaning of "harmony."
  ◆ Ask, "How are we serving those around us when we live in, or promote, harmony?"
- As students ink in the page, present the following example from the life of Jesus:

  The Pharisees continued to try to trick Jesus. They hoped to prove that He was not God. One day they asked Him a question about paying taxes, thinking that His answer would break a law of God. *Read Luke 20:20-26 to your class.*

  The answer Jesus gave them showed His willingness to live in harmony with human government because it is separate from God's government. *Discuss other ways Jesus showed His willingness to follow the rules of human government.* If desired, ask "Does this mean that God approves of every decision and rule made by government?"

  ◆ Compare the command to live in harmony with other believers with Jesus' statement that a belief in Him may cause division within a family (Mark 10:29-31).
- Call on students to recite the portion of the theme verse you have learned so far.

59 DILIGENCE

- Present trait information.
  ◆ Discuss the verse and the affect of diligence on those around us.
  ◆ Review past traits and verses.
  ◆ Drill creatively to encourage memorization of this unit's information.
- Errand-Running Hazards
  ◆ Call on a student to recite the verse for diligence.
  ◆ Consider what qualities in Darcie would make it easy to predict that she would have difficulty refusing distractions in delivering a message.
  ◆ Instruct students to title hazards in the maze, imagining the kinds of distractions Darcie might encounter. Show your pleasure over their creativity.

Use the following anecdote – as well as the one on the next page – to strengthen the concept of diligence to your students:

Messenger Anecdote One

During World War II, General George Patton was given command of an American armored unit in North Africa. He wanted desperately to be victorious in his first encounter with the Germans, commanded by Rommel. As the battle began, he tried to contact one of the supporting units on a field phone. The phone would not work properly. The battle might be lost unless he could make contact, so he sent his trusted aide, Dick, over to

UNIT SIX
Serving by Getting Along With Others

"Live in harmony with one another." Romans 12:16

DILIGENCE ◆ PATIENCE ◆ THOROUGHNESS

Definition: Doing my work steadily until it is done.

DILIGENCE
Serving by Finishing What I Start

Opposite: Quitting when I feel like it.

Bible words:
"Like the coolness of the snow at harvest time is a trustworthy messenger to those who send him; he refreshes the spirit of his masters." Proverbs 25:13

ERRAND-RUNNING HAZARDS

Being a diligent messenger means overcoming hazards along the way. Darcie has been asked to deliver a message to her mother's best friend who is at the park with her small children. Find the shortest path to the park. Title each hazard in the maze of people and things that you feel might tempt Darcie to stop her errand-running.

Ex.: Grandma's House

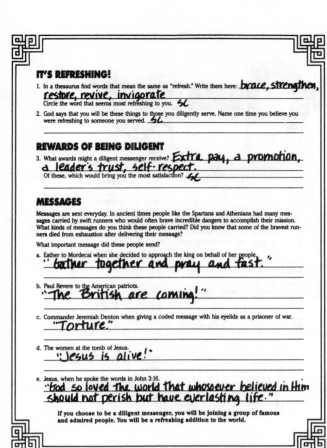

IT'S REFRESHING!

1. In a thesaurus find words that mean the same as "refresh." Write them here: *brace, strengthen, restore, revive, invigorate*
Circle the word that seems most refreshing to you. *SC*

2. God says that you will be these things to those you diligently serve. Name one time you believe you were refreshing to someone you served. *SC*

REWARDS OF BEING DILIGENT

3. What awards might a diligent messenger receive? *Extra pay, a promotion, a leader's trust, self-respect.*
Of these, which would bring you the most satisfaction? *SC*

MESSAGES

Messages are sent everyday. In ancient times people like the Spartans and Athenians had many messages carried by swift runners who would often brave incredible dangers to accomplish their mission. What kinds of messages do you think these people carried? Did you know that some of the bravest runners died from exhaustion after delivering their message?

What important message did these people send?

a. Esther to Mordecai when she decided to approach the king on behalf of her people.
"Gather together and pray and fast."

b. Paul Revere to the American patriots.
"The British are coming!"

c. Commander Jeremiah Denton when giving a coded message with his eyelids as a prisoner of war.
"Torture."

d. The women at the tomb of Jesus.
"Jesus is alive!"

e. Jesus, when he spoke the words in John 3:16.
"God so loved the world that whosoever believed in Him should not perish but have everlasting life."

If you choose to be a diligent messenger, you will be joining a group of famous and admired people. You will be a refreshing addition to the world.

Haman leads Mordecai through the streets.

the supporting unit's position. Dick braved heavy enemy fire as he drove his jeep rapidly over the desert hillocks. He reached the American flanking unit and delivered the message from General Patton. Just as he was about to leave, however, a German bomber strafed his position, killing him instantly. General Patton was deeply grieved by the loss of his loyal aide, but felt great pride in the knowledge that in faithfully delivering the message, Dick had helped win the important battle.

60 IT'S REFRESHING

- Complete 1-3. Compare and discuss answers.
- Messages
  - Recall these historical messages.
  - Call on students to give answers to the class.
  - Extend the activity by discussing the risks involved in each situation. Encourage students to imagine being the messenger and facing the dangers, then experiencing the satisfaction of completing the assignment.

SPIN-OFF

FAMOUS MESSAGES. Divide your class into five small groups. Assign each group a message from those on SP 60. On a thick pad of small scrap or note paper, each group will design, draw, and caption an "animated" tablet cartoon depicting the event and the message.

Messenger Anecdote Two

A group of students set out on a daylight climb of Mt. Hood, a beautiful mountain in Oregon. The weather was fine and there seemed to be nothing to worry about. A few turned back and returned early because of fatigue, but the rest forged ahead, climbing steadily in the clear, cold air. Before reaching the summit, something totally unexpected happened. A freak spring storm struck the mountain with a fury that left the group dazed, frightened, and confused. The leader knew that unless they acted quickly they might all perish. He instructed the students to dig snow caves that would provide some protection against the storm, and told them to wait there until he could bring help. Braving the swirling wind and snow, he struggled back down the mountain, hoping he would have the strength and good fortune to reach those who would begin the rescue of the trapped students. His hopes were realized when, after many hours, he was able to deliver his message. The rescue began, and two of the students were found alive in the snow cave.

Serve your students by diligently delivering God's message of love.

61 ESTHER ILLUSTRATION

- Examine the picture with your class.
  - Note the emotion of the scene.

62 BACKFIRE: Episode Six Of The Esther Story

- Update one another on past episodes of the story.
- Read the story individually or together.
  ▶ Allow the irony of the situation to stimulate a lively discussion about the unlikelihood that the reading of the history books on the eve of Mordecai's scheduled death was a "coincidence." Comment on the unseen hand of God upon the lives of His children.

 SPIN-OFF

GOD'S UNSEEN HAND. Tell the class a true story from your own experience or that of another person which demonstrates God's active participation "behind the scenes." An example: Some builders were remodeling a basement while the owners of the home were away. One morning, shortly after the builders arrived, a cord shorted out and began smoldering on the family room carpet. Soon the room was filled with smoke, and flames were beginning to crawl up the wall. The builders "just happened" to open the family room door in time to put out the flames and save the home from destruction. Collect similar stories from your students by asking them to write their true story in a paragraph. Read them to the class, one or two at a time, throughout the unit.

63 BACK TO BACKFIRE

- Complete the page.
  ▶ 1-3. Consider and rank reasons for eagerness to go to Heaven. Discuss answers.

EPISODE SIX

ESTHER

BACK FIRE

The king's curiosity kept him from sleeping well that night. With every toss and turn of his body, Xerxes tried to guess what favor Esther was going to request. "Maybe she wants me to build her a new library! No. Maybe she wants to take a long vacation!"

When he ran out of ideas about Esther, and was still not asleep, Xerxes woke up his servants. "Read me the record books," he said. The king was sure that the reading of history would put him to sleep. But, like any good history book, it intrigued rather than bored him. Of special interest to him was the part about a man who uncovered a plot to kill the king.

"Has that man Mordecai been rewarded for his loyalty to me?" asked the king.

"No. Nothing has been done for him," answered his attendants.

By this time, the sun was up. Haman was already entering the king's court. He wanted Mordecai to have an early hanging.

When King Xerxes heard someone in the court, he said, "Who is outside?" His servants answered, "Haman."

"Send him in," ordered the king excitedly. Before Haman could say a word, the king began speaking to him. "Haman, what should I do for someone I want to honor?"

"Well," thought Haman, "isn't it grand of the king to want to honor me!" Haman let his imagination carry him to his finest idea. "I suggest that the king honor this person by placing him on one of the king's own royal horses – the kind with the king's crest on it. The honored one should wear a robe that the king himself has worn. Next, one of the king's prized servants should lead the man through the streets of the city shouting, 'This is the man the king wants to honor!'"

Haman was proud of himself for coming up with such a glorious plan. He rubbed his hands together, eager

for his one-man parade to begin. He imagined that he could feel the luxury of the king's robes on his shoulders already.

The king agreed with Haman that his idea was brilliant. "Perfect! Perfect! And that is precisely what I want you to do for Mordecai, the Jew. You know, the one who sits at the palace gate."

Haman's mouth dried up and his cheeks twitched. His breath came out in short puffs, and he shook his head to be sure his ears were working. "I couldn't have heard what I think I heard," he thought.

"Hurry up!" said the king. "I want Mordecai to be in my robe and on that horse in less than an hour!"

"It's true, then," mumbled Haman. Rage replaced his shock. Haman slowly realized that Mordecai would be the man honored instead of him and that it would be Mordecai who would be placed upon the king's horse instead of upon Haman's gallows.

Haman walked Mordecai through the streets of the town with legs that felt like lead. Each step added another lump to his throat and another layer to his humiliation. When the ordeal was over and the people of the town knew that the king had honored Mordecai, Haman ran home and covered his head in embarrassment.

His family and friends gathered around him. "Mordecai has started your downfall," they said. "On top of that, he is a Jew. There is no way you will stand against him!" Even in their foolishness, Haman's wife and friends were wise enough to know that the God of Israel is more powerful than anyone's wicked schemes.

While his wife and friends were still serving doomish thoughts to Haman, the servants of the king arrived to whisk him away to Esther's second banquet. He was hardly hungry.

BACK TO BACK FIRE

BACKFIRE 6

1. How did King Xerxes try to get to sleep after worrying about Esther's request?
   By listening to a servant read him the history books.

2. What reminded him of his earlier desire to reward Mordecai for loyalty?
   When the servant read about the plot that Mordecai uncovered.

3. Draw four pictures of Haman's face. The first should show him waiting outside the king's door, the second should show him listening to what he thought the king was going to do for him, the third should show him at the moment he realized whom the king was really talking about, and the fourth should show him as he led Mordecai around the town.

   Student draws Haman's face.

4. What would have been your recommendation to the king for honoring a person who demonstrated great loyalty?
   SC

5. Describe the details of the way in which King Xerxes was going to honor Mordecai.
   Lead him through the streets on King's horse, wearing King's robe, saying "This is the man the King honors."

6. List any parts of this episode that demonstrated initiative, patience, or thoroughness by the characters.
   SC

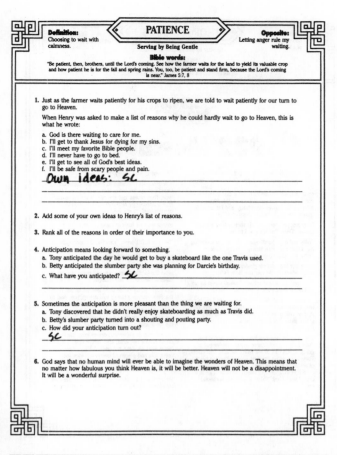

PATIENCE

Definition: Choosing to wait with calmness.

Opposite: Letting anger rule my waiting.

Serving by Being Gentle

Bible words:
"Be patient, then, brothers, until the Lord's coming. See how the farmer waits for the land to yield its valuable crop and how patient he is for the fall and spring rains. You, too, be patient and stand firm, because the Lord's coming is near." James 5:7, 8

1. Just as the farmer waits patiently for his crops to ripen, we are told to wait patiently for our turn to go to Heaven.

   When Henry was asked to make a list of reasons why he could hardly wait to go to Heaven, this is what he wrote:
   a. God is there waiting to care for me.
   b. I'll get to thank Jesus for dying for my sins.
   c. I'll meet my favorite Bible people.
   d. I'll never have to go to bed.
   e. I'll get to see all of God's best ideas.
   f. I'll be safe from scary people and pain.

   Own ideas: SC

2. Add some of your own ideas to Henry's list of reasons.

3. Rank all of the reasons in order of their importance to you.

4. Anticipation means looking forward to something.
   a. Tony anticipated the day he would get to buy a skateboard like the one Travis used.
   b. Betty anticipated the slumber party she was planning for Darcie's birthday.
   c. What have you anticipated? _SC_

5. Sometimes the anticipation is more pleasant than the thing we are waiting for.
   a. Tony discovered that he didn't really enjoy skateboarding as much as Travis did.
   b. Betty's slumber party turned into a shouting and pouting party.
   c. How did your anticipation turn out?
   _SC_

6. God says that no human mind will ever be able to imagine the wonders of Heaven. This means that no matter how fabulous you think Heaven is, it will be better. Heaven will not be a disappointment. It will be a wonderful surprise.

HEAVENLY TREASURES

In Matthew 6:19-21 Jesus advises us to spend our time building up our treasury in Heaven. This is one wise thing we can do while we wait patiently to go there ourselves.

Knowing what you know of God, what three actions do you believe would build the most treasure in Heaven?

Ex: 1. _Loving God._
2. _Following Jesus._
3. _Loving, serving others._

Choose one of the activities and design a Treasury Certificate of Heaven. List the action, state its value, and decorate it in a heavenly way! As you do this, imagine yourself in Heaven opening your treasury vault and finding it full. How can that thought become true? It's up to you.

Ex:

TREASURY CERTIFICATE OF HEAVEN
in the amount of
$ _100.00_
awarded to
Monica
for
following Jesus by sharing her lunch with a hungry and lonely classmate.
Date
January 12

64 PATIENCE

● Read and drill trait information.
  ◗ Review past traits and verses.
● Complete page.
  ◗ 1-3. Consider and rank reasons for eagerness to go to Heaven. Discuss answers.
  ◗ 4-5. Discuss things students have anticipated and their results.

 SPIN-OFF

WAYS OF WAITING. Use the trait verse as a springboard for an imaginative exercise in similes. Ask students to write a sentence about waiting that is similar in style to the second sentence of the verse. **Invite them to illustrate their simile. Post on the board for all to enjoy.**

65 HEAVENLY TREASURES

● Instruct students to consider three acts that they believe are especially commendable in God's sight. Encourage individuality of thought.
  ◗ Following the activity, discuss the various ideas and values of the deeds.
● Close the session by considering how patience increases our ability to serve others well. Ex: Allows those we serve to feel relaxed around us; gives us more time to find ways to help.

Serve your students with a calm and patient spirit.

The Project Servant suggestions for this unit may be found on page 93 of this book.

66 THOROUGHNESS: SERVANT STORY AND INTERMISSION

- Read and review trait information and verse.
- Use the following anecdote to introduce the quality of thoroughness:

Thoroughness Anecdote

The hearts of all Americans grieved when the news of the Space Shuttle tragedy reached them. The death of the seven astronauts was totally unexpected and incredible. What went wrong? Could the accident have been prevented? The Presidential Commission set up to study the tragedy discovered some revealing and sobering facts. One of the O-rings that sealed the joints between the tanks of the external rocket boosters did not function properly. This allowed a fiery plume of flame to burn into the main engine of the shuttle, causing a massive explosion. Some felt that the O-ring failed because the shuttle was launched in very cold weather, with temperatures in the thirties. The company that made the O-rings and the rocket boosters said that the rings were theoretically good down to 25 degrees. However, the Commission pressed them even more closely about this and discovered that the rings were never actually tested down to these low temperatures. A lack of thoroughness may have led to one of America's most tragic moments.

- Read story and discuss.

 SPIN-OFF

THOROUGHNESS THEORIES. Challenge students to discover other historical and contemporary events that have been affected by thoroughness or a lack of it. Make a list identifying and supporting their conclusions. Display.

Serve your students by being thorough in your evaluation of them.

67 STORY, CONTINUED, AND FOLLOW-UP QUESTIONS

- Follow-up questions:
1. What game was being played when Henry came up with his good idea? [Monopoly.]
2. Describe his idea. [That everyone in their sixth grade class should get a word of love on Valentine's Day.]
3. How was the idea broadened and by whom? [To include both sixth grades by Darcie; to fifth and sixth grades by Betty; to the whole school by David.]
4. What was the card to look like? [Tri-fold on colored paper, computer-printed, with a picture drawn by Henry on the front.] What might have been its message? [Student choice.]
5. Why do you think Darcie had trouble thinking clearly about things like math around David? [Student choice. Suggestions: David expected her to be incompetent about those things; she cared too greatly about his opinion of her.]
6. What was Tony's main concern, or fear about the project? [That they would not be able to complete it on time.] What influences might have contributed to his fears? [Student choice. Suggestions: Past failures; own cautious temperament; overtiredness; lack of confidence in the idea.]
7. To what "bumpy road" of God's was Tony referring to in the last line of the story? [Jesus' life and death on earth.]
8. What were some of the bumps in the life of Jesus? [Pharisees; disciples who deserted Him; family and friends who misunderstood Him; general lack of understanding from those around Him; Satan's temptations; persecutions and death.]
9. What does it tell you about God that He chose love to be the greatest power in the world? [Student choice.]

Definition: Completing the details of a task.

◆ **THOROUGHNESS** ◆

Opposite: Overlooking the details of a task.

Serving by Taking Care of Details

Bible words:
"The Lord will fulfill His purpose for me; Your love, O Lord, endures forever – do not abandon the works of Your hands." Psalm 138:8

 SERVANT STORY

932 Messages

Somewhere between the time the Monopoly game began and the moment Tony bought hotels for St. Charles Place, Henry had a good idea. "I think that we should make sure that everyone in our class gets a word of love on Valentine's Day. After all, God loves everybody, and I'm sure He would like us to remind them of it."

Tony stopped counting his money long enough to say, "Okay. Sounds good to me."

"Why just our class?" asked Darcie the following day at school when Henry told her his idea. "Why not both sixth grades?"

"Why not fifth and six grades?" asked Betty at lunch when Darcie told her Henry's idea.

"Why not the whole school?" asked David as he and Betty were walking to choir.

"Why not?" said Henry when he heard how his idea had grown. "I'd like to draw the picture on it, if no one minds." Henry's confidence had grown since last September when he broke his leg.

The time left between Henry's idea and Valentine's Day was only three weeks. "We've got to get going on this or we won't make it," cautioned Tony. They spent the first week gathering names of students and teachers. "I don't believe how hard it is to figure out exactly who is in each class," said Tony. "What if we leave someone out?"

"We won't," said Henry. "You'll see."

The group had decided to print the cards on David's computer using colored paper and fancy type. They would fold the card three times and glue a photocopy of Henry's drawing on the front of each card. "Let's see," said Darcie. "There are 874 kids in our school and 58 teachers. That means that we have to make . . . uh . . . 922 Valentines!"

"No, not 922, Darcie," said David impatiently. "It's 932, which means that each of us is responsible for 187 Valentines."

"186.40 to be exact," said Darcie, hoping to surprise David. "For some reason I never do well in math around him."

Once the group chose their favorite sketch from the three samples Henry had drawn, they had to decide what to say inside the card. Everyone had a different idea. Two days went by without a decision. On the third day, Tony said, "Let's put the ideas into a bowl and draw one out."

Darcie's slip of paper was drawn from the bowl. David read it out loud, and Darcie said, "I don't like it after all. Let's not use it." They ended up using bits and pieces of everyone's idea for the message inside the cards, but deciding to do that took another day.

"At least we care about what we say on the card," said Henry, looking at the cheery side of things.

"Let's hope that caring doesn't take so long next time," said Tony. "We only have eleven days left."

That afternoon David announced to the group that he had entered the message and the format for the card into the computer. It's ready to print!" Everyone cheered.

The next morning, David didn't want to talk to anyone. It took Betty's special way of caring to find out from him that his father had copied another program over the disk with the Valentine project on it. "He thought it was a blank disk because I hadn't taken the time to put a label on it," said David in a hopeless-sounding way.

The group tried not to groan loud enough for David to hear when Betty passed them the bad news. "Shall we quit this whole thing?" asked Tony.

"Maybe," said Darcie.

"I don't know," said Betty.

"No!" said Henry. "We're not going to let a few little bumps knock us off the road!" The group liked the way Henry used words. "Besides, I just thought of something."

"What?" asked Tony.

"Jesus ran into some giant bumps in the road when He was trying to deliver God's message of love to the world, so why should we let a few little ones stop us," said Henry with excitement. "We can do it. We can. Come on!" He led the group over to David, who gradually left his blues behind and agreed to re-program the message and format on a labelled disk.

On the fifth night before Valentine's Day, another set-back hit the project. "Where's the picture I

left on the coffee table last night," asked Henry in the morning. He heard one "I didn't take it" followed by six "Me neithers." The one member of the family that didn't answer him was the one in the corner sleeping on pieces of shredded paper. Jerome's playfulness had caused another bump in the road.

Tony couldn't believe it when Henry reluctantly told him the upsetting news. "But I'll draw another one tonight," he said.

"Tonight is too late, Henry," said Tony. "I was supposed to take it to the print shop today." The two boys came up with a compromise plan. "You go home right after school and draw another picture and I'll deliver your papers," said Tony. "It'll feel good to do the route again anyway."

Before the boys had a chance to talk about Saturday's game, Betty and Darcie ran up to them and said, "Tony, cross Joey North and Teddy Smith off your list, and, Henry, add Sa Joon Le. The boys are moving to another city and Sa Joon is a new girl from another country." Tony just shook his head. "These bumps are a little too bumpy for me, Henry." The others chuckled at him.

When Valentine's Day arrived and the cards were delivered, Tony decided that the bumps had been worth it. Even his writing hand seemed to hurt less once he saw the cards being read.

"Pretty good idea, Henry," said Tony as he opened his own card. When he read it, he felt as though God Himself was giving him a message of love. "Thanks," he whispered, "for not giving up when the road got bumpy for You."

INTER**MISSION**

Pretend you are as discouraged as David was. What might a caring person like Betty do or say to help you?

◼ NEXT-TIME NOTES
to make next time better

SP 58: _____

SP 59: _____

SP 60: _____

SP 61: _____

SP 62: _____

SP 63: _____

SP 64: _____

SP 65: _____

SP 66: _____

SP 67: _____

PROJECT SERVANT: _____

OTHER: _____

◼ AFTERTHOUGHTS
Thoughts too good to lose • Kidquotes • Thoughts from God • Ideas

_____

_____

_____

_____

_____

_____

☝ STEP ONE

Forgiveness is one of those treasures in the Christian stockpile that is admired but seldom chosen. Perhaps that is because in order to reach it we must climb over the high, barbed wall called pride. Pride positions itself between us and forgiveness because it knows that nothing demolishes walls quite like forgiveness.

However, for those of us who risk the climb over pride and grab the treasure of forgiveness, there is an explosion of peace, a God-quake which rattles every corner of our lives with the quiet hum of freedom.

Jesus was a master at wiping the sin slate clean. He repeatedly showed us how to treat sin: address it, then forget it. How odd that seems to us. Odd and impossible.

When Jesus warmly greeted Peter and unguardedly carried on their friendship after Peter had betrayed Him, Jesus set the standard for us. Treating those who have wronged us as if they had not is a hefty order. It means we must get rid of our mental tally of who did what. It also means we must give up the pleasures of unforgiveness which make our fingers and tongues wag and our pride swell.

As those who claim to walk with God, it is critical that we accurately model His forgiveness. "Love keeps no record of wrongs" is a clear challenge to live above unforgiveness. Instead of "Forgive? Okay. Forget? No way!" let's live God's way. Wipe the slate clean, and teach to the accompaniment of that quiet hum of freedom.

> In my mind
> God and I drew two pictures
> Of all the wrong I had done.
>
> On my page
> Ugly sins filled the paper.
> On God's page
> There was not even one.
>
> In my mind
> God and I talked it over.
> I said, "Lord, how can this be true?"
>
> He said, "Child,
> do you not understand yet?
> I've paid for the sin that you do."

PATTERNING

Is there someone in your class still suffering emotional cut-off from you because they did wrong? Do they sense in you a mistrust or write-off? Speak to God about it and ask Him to help you forgive as He forgives, as if you have never been wronged. Unforgiveness is as much a sin as anything our students can do.

CHEWABLES
Bite-sized thoughts from God's Word

Select one thought to "chew on" during this unit:

"If You, O Lord, kept a record of sins, O Lord, who could stand? But with You there is forgiveness; therefore You are feared." Psalm 130:3, 4

"And what I have forgiven – if there was anything to forgive – I have forgiven in the sight of Christ for your sake, in order that Satan might not outwit us. For we are not unaware of his schemes." 2 Corinthians 2:10, 11

"Love keeps no record of wrongs." 1 Corinthians 13:5

UNIT INFORMATION

Theme Verse:
Romans 12:16
"Do not be proud, but be willing to associate with people of low position."

Esther Study:
Esther dramatically reveals Haman's plot to the king.

PART A: FORGIVENESS

Purpose:
To demonstrate the futility of holding a grudge.

To give an example of where one man's grudge led him.

Approach:
Revenge is a natural feeling; forgiveness is super-natural. Grudges do harm to the grudge-holder.

Definition:
Caring more about God than my grudge.

Opposite:
Caring more about my grudge than about God.

Trait Verse:
Proverbs 20:22
"Do not say, 'I'll pay you back for this wrong!' Wait for the Lord, and He will deliver you."

Visual Reinforcement:
Invite students to illustrate and write a commentary on their idea of a grudge.

Ask some students to volunteer to create an attractive poster displaying the unit's subtitle (Serving by Accepting People) and theme verse. Display it conspicuously.

Ideas:
To help students get an idea of the amount of sin God forgives daily, instruct students to compile a class list of common sins committed by people in general. Multiply the list times the approximate number of people in your school, city, county, nation, and world. Multiply this figure by the number of days in a year, decade, century, and so on. Stop to thank God for His forgiveness. Use the exercise to also consider our responsibility not to take advantage of God's grace.

Use as Desired:
SP 70, My Photo Album
SP 72, Reversing the Decree

PART B: FAIRNESS

Purpose:
To define judicial terms.

To present cases needing fair judgments.

Approach:
Solomon received wisdom from God which allowed him to judge thousands of situations fairly. God can also give me wisdom to determine justice.

Definition:
Judging a situation fairly.

Opposite:
Showing favorites in my decisions.

Trait Verse:
Proverbs 18:5
"It is not good to be partial to the wicked or to deprive the innocent of justice."

Visual Reinforcement:
Visualize the trait verse and place on a bulletin board. Add clippings of court proceedings from newspapers and magazines as well as any official documents from an attorney or judge.

Ideas:
Keep track of Supreme Court proceedings, as well as local and regional decisions. Are the courts being "partial to the wicked"? Are they "depriving the innocent of justice"? Write letters of praise to judges making wise decisions, and letters of protest to judges making unwise, or ungodly, decisions.

Use as Desired:
SP 74, Court in Session

PART C: FRIENDLINESS

Purpose:
To provide the student with an example of friendliness in story form.

Approach:
There are those around me needing a friend. When I am a friend, I will have a better chance at having a friend.

Definition:
Reaching out to others in a warm-hearted way.

Opposite:
Responding to others with coolness.

Trait Verse:
Proverbs 27:9
"Perfume and incense bring joy to the heart, and the pleasantness of one's friend springs from his earnest counsel."

Visual Reinforcement:
Make up a slogan for friendliness. Ask an artistic person to make it into a class logo, then use it as a T-shirt transfer, a letterhead for friendly letters, or a giant poster.

Ideas:
Analyze the Servant Group in the servant stories. Note how each has served the others as a friend. Do the same for other stories your class is reading.

Use as Desired:
SP 76, The Best Friend
TG 94, Project Servant: Friendliness

MY PLAN FOR THIS UNIT

_____

_____

_____

_____

68 INTRO TO UNIT

- Read through text.
- Review past portions of the theme verse.
  - ◆ Add this unit's verse.
  - ◆ Drill for memory.
- Discuss the meaning of "accepting" people.
  - ◆ Ask, "How are we serving people when we accept them?"
- Ink in the page.
  - ◆ As students ink in the page, ask them to think over the life of Jesus and name the many types and kinds of people with whom He associated. Thumb through the gospels to locate additional examples of His acceptance of all types of people.
  - ◆ Consider with your class the difference between accepting people and condoning their behavior.
  - ◆ Stimulate student thinking by asking, "If accepting a person is the first step, what is the second?"
  - ◆ Also, "Most of the people who met Jesus changed from their life of sin to a life of doing good. What does this say about the source of real change in a person?"

UNIT SEVEN
Serving by
Accepting People

"Do not be proud, but be willing to associate with people of low position."
Romans 12:16

FORGIVENESS ◆ FAIRNESS ◆ FRIENDSHIP

69 FORGIVENESS

- Present trait information.
  - ◆ Discuss the verse and the idea of revenge.
  - ◆ Lead the class in a lively review of past traits and verses.
- Revenge
  - ◆ Read and complete.
  - ◆ Discuss answers, seeking to convey the futility of grudges.
- Thinking Things Over
  - ◆ Complete this section, analyzing the ingredients and affects of grudge-holding and forgiveness.
- Absalom – The Grudge Holder
  - ◆ Read the paragraphs.
  - ◆ Instruct students to look up the assigned reference and write the outcome of Absalom's grudge in a complete sentence.
  - ◆ Consider how circumstances could have been different if Absalom had "stepped aside" to let God deal with the problem.

Serve your students by forgiving them thoroughly.

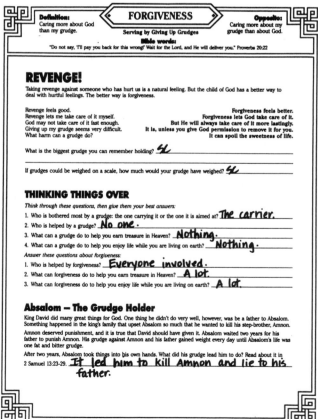

Definition: Caring more about God than my grudge.

FORGIVENESS
Serving by Giving Up Grudges

Opposite: Caring more about my grudge than about God.

Bible words:
"Do not say, 'I'll pay you back for this wrong!' Wait for the Lord, and He will deliver you." Proverbs 20:22

REVENGE!

Taking revenge against someone who has hurt us is a natural feeling. But the child of God has a better way to deal with hurtful feelings. The better way is forgiveness.

Revenge feels good.
Revenge lets me take care of it myself.
God may not take care of it fast enough.
Giving up my grudge seems very difficult.
What harm can a grudge do?

Forgiveness feels better.
Forgiveness lets God take care of it.
But He will always take care of it more lastingly.
It is, unless you give God permission to remove it for you.
It can spoil the sweetness of life.

What is the biggest grudge you can remember holding? *SL* _____

If grudges could be weighed on a scale, how much would your grudge have weighed? *SL* _____

THINKING THINGS OVER

Think through these questions, then give them your best answers:
1. Who is bothered most by a grudge: the one carrying it or the one it is aimed at? **The carrier.**
2. Who is helped by a grudge? **No one.**
3. What can a grudge do to help you earn treasure in Heaven? **Nothing.**
4. What can a grudge do to help you enjoy life while you are living on earth? **Nothing.**

Answer these questions about forgiveness:
1. Who is helped by forgiveness? **Everyone involved.**
2. What can forgiveness do to help you earn treasure in Heaven? **A lot.**
3. What can forgiveness do to help you enjoy life while you are living on earth? **A lot.**

Absalom — The Grudge Holder

King David did many great things for God. One thing he didn't do very well, however, was be a father to Absalom. Something happened in the king's family that upset Absalom so much that he wanted to kill his step-brother, Amnon.

Amnon deserved punishment, and it is true that David should have given it. Absalom waited two years for his father to punish Amnon. His grudge against Amnon and his father gained weight every day until Absalom's life was one fat and bitter grudge.

After two years, Absalom took things into his own hands. What did his grudge lead him to do? Read about it in 2 Samuel 13:23-29. **It led him to kill Amnon and lie to his father.**

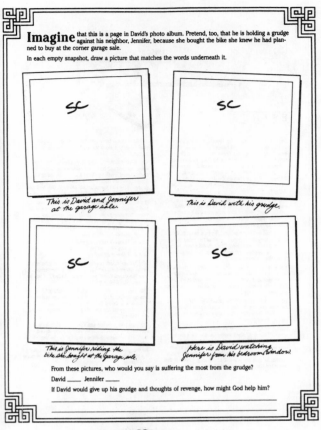

Imagine that this is a page in David's photo album. Pretend, too, that he is holding a grudge against his neighbor, Jennifer, because she bought the bike she knew he had planned to buy at the corner garage sale.

In each empty snapshot, draw a picture that matches the words underneath it.

This is David and Jennifer at the garage sale.

This is David with his grudge.

This is Jennifer riding the bike she bought at the garage sale.

Here is David watching Jennifer from his bedroom window.

From these pictures, who would you say is suffering the most from the grudge?

David _____ Jennifer _____

If David would give up his grudge and thoughts of revenge, how might God help him?

_____

70 PHOTO ALBUM

● Complete the page as indicated.
 ▶ Follow the activity with a display of student work.
 ▶ Discuss student ideas about ways God could intervene in a situation like David's if he were willing to forgive.
 ▶ Seek to help students understand the idea of "stepping aside" and letting God deal with those who wrong us. Ask, "Who would do a better job of teaching someone an important lesson: God or you?"

 SPIN-OFF
MY PHOTO ALBUM. Instruct students to design a page similar to SP 70 to illustrate a grudge they have held.

71 ESTHER ILLUSTRATION

● Examine the picture with your class.
 ▶ Call on students to suggest words that describe the emotions of everyone in the picture.

Haman sprawled across Esther in the banquet room.

72 BACKFIRE: Episode Seven Of The Esther Story

- Review past episodes.
- Read the story.
  - ▶ Discuss the exciting turn of events.
  - ▶ Encourage students to look for God's role in the story.

 SPIN-OFF

REVERSING THE DECREE. Invite students to sit in the place of Esther and Mordecai by composing a decree that will save the Jews from destruction without overturning the king's first decree. If desired, students may write their decree on parchment-like paper and post on a bulletin board.

73 BACK TO BACKFIRE

- Complete the follow-up questions.
  - ▶ Discuss answers, leaving room for differences of opinion.

ESTHER

EPISODE SEVEN

BACK FIRE

The ride to the palace was too short for Haman. He needed more time to get himself ready to pretend everything was all right. "How can I sit at a dinner with Xerxes and Esther knowing that Mordecai has just made a fool out of me in front of the entire city!" He tried to comfort himself by thinking ahead to the thirteenth of Adar, the day the Jews would be slaughtered. "At least I will have the last laugh," he thought.

The king waited impatiently for Haman to arrive. He was tired of being curious about Esther's request, and he didn't want to lose another night's sleep over it. When Haman arrived, the two troubled men hurried to Esther's banquet room.

Esther had ordered her maids to fix a meal fit for a king. As they ate, however, none of the three diners tasted much of their food. Their mouths were talking about the weather and politics, but their minds were telling them other things.

The king kept wishing dinner were over so he could ask Esther to name her request. Haman's thoughts raced back and forth between doom and glory, and Esther rehearsed the exact words of her request over and over in her mind.

When dinner was over, the anxious king blurted out his curiosity. "So, Esther, I ask you again. What is it you want? Remember, you may have anything up to half of my kingdom."

Esther changed positions as she readied herself to speak. "This is it," she thought. As she took a deep breath, she could feel her courage mounting. The king leaned toward her, eagerly waiting to hear her words. Haman left his thoughts about Mordecai long enough to copy the interest of the king. Anything that interested the king interested Haman, or so he pretended.

"If I have found favor with the king, and if it pleases your majesty, I plead for my life and the life of my people."

King Xerxes looked confused. Not one of his ideas about her request had even come close to this! He hadn't heard anything about Esther's life being in danger. Haman, on the other hand, was feeling a strange quiver in the pit of his stomach that had nothing to do with the leg of lamb he had just eaten.

"I and my people have been sold to be slaughtered," said Esther. She tried hard to control the pace of her words but they began pushing themselves out quickly. "If we had merely been sold as slaves, I would have kept quiet, because no such distress would have been reason enough to bother you."

By now, Haman's quivering stomach was swirling like an angry sea. "It can't be," he thought. "Esther can't be a Jew! She can't be!"

King Xerxes stood, hoping that by standing he would better understand her words. "Who is the person who has dared to sell your people, Esther?" Then he demanded, "Who is he?"

This was the moment all Israel was waiting for. It was up to Esther to make it work. Haman was overcome with a dread that seemed to paralyze him. "The man who wants me and my people destroyed is this vile Haman!"

The king was shocked and spun around to look at Haman. It was too much for him to grasp in one moment. He furiously stomped outside to the garden to gather his thoughts. As Haman watched the king head for the garden, there was no doubt in his mind that the king was going to put him to death. His only hope was Esther.

Every piece of pride melted away from Haman.

Nothing mattered to him now except saving his own life. He threw himself across the queen and begged her to save him. At that moment, the king returned to the banquet room. "Oh, I see. I leave you for just a moment and you try to molest my queen!"

"No! No! That isn't it!" cried Haman, but it was too late for words to make a difference. The guards grabbed him and covered his head. On the way out of the room, one of them said, "There is a set of gallows seventy-five feet high at Haman's house. He had them built for Mordecai."

Then, just as his wife and friends had predicted, Haman heard the words of doom. "Hang Haman on those gallows!" When word reached the king that his orders had been carried out, his fury subsided. Xerxes gave all of Haman's land and wealth to Esther, who put Mordecai in charge of it.

Esther's plan had worked, but one problem remained: the king could not take back a decree signed with his ring. Esther had stopped Haman, but now something had to be done to stop the slaughter.

 BACK TO BACK FIRE

BACKFIRE 7

1. Why did Haman believe that he was going to have the last laugh?
   Because of the slaughter he had planned for the Jews.

2. Describe Esther's feelings as she prepared to tell the king of her request.
   SC

3. What was her request? How did it differ from what the king and Haman thought she was going to ask?
   For help in sparing her life. They expected her to ask for things or property.

4. Haman obviously didn't do his homework about Esther. What one fact about her background did he overlook, not knowing that it would lead to his death?
   That she, too, was a Jew.

5. After Haman realized the deadly peril he was in, he threw himself at the mercy of Esther. If she had had time to consider his sorry state, do you think she would have forgiven him? Do you think she should have forgiven him?
   SC

6. One of the qualities of a good king is fairness. Do you think King Xerxes was fair in his punishment of Haman?
   SC

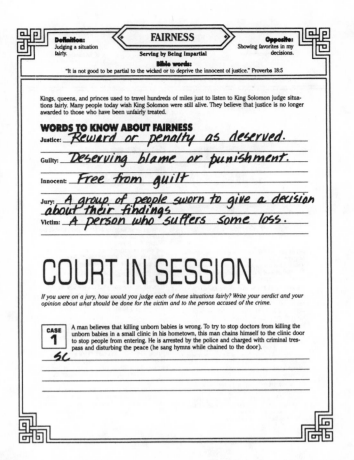

Kings, queens, and princes used to travel hundreds of miles just to listen to King Solomon judge situations fairly. Many people today wish King Solomon were still alive. They believe that justice is no longer awarded to those who have been unfairly treated.

WORDS TO KNOW ABOUT FAIRNESS

Justice: *Reward or penalty as deserved.*

Guilty: *Deserving blame or punishment.*

Innocent: *Free from guilt*

Jury: *A group of people sworn to give a decision about their findings*

Victim: *A person who suffers some loss.*

COURT IN SESSION

If you were on a jury, how would you judge each of these situations fairly? Write your verdict and your opinion about what should be done for the victim and to the person accused of the crime.

CASE 1
A man believes that killing unborn babies is wrong. To try to stop doctors from killing the unborn babies in a small clinic in his hometown, this man chains himself to the clinic door to stop people from entering. He is arrested by the police and charged with criminal trespass and disturbing the peace (he sang hymns while chained to the door).

SC

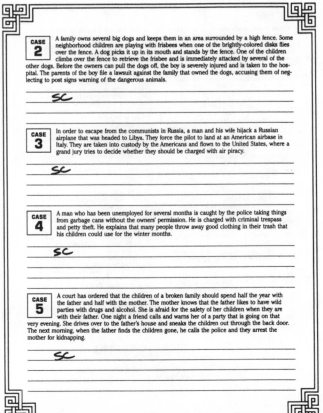

CASE 2
A family owns several big dogs and keeps them in an area surrounded by a high fence. Some neighborhood children are playing with frisbees when one of the brightly-colored disks flies over the fence. A dog picks it up in its mouth and stands by the fence. One of the children climbs over the fence to retrieve the frisbee and is immediately attacked by several of the other dogs. Before the owners can pull the dogs off, the boy is severely injured and is taken to the hospital. The parents of the boy file a lawsuit against the family that owned the dogs, accusing them of neglecting to post signs warning of the dangerous animals.

SC

CASE 3
In order to escape from the communists in Russia, a man and his wife hijack a Russian airplane that was headed to Libya. They force the pilot to land at an American airbase in Italy. They are taken into custody by the Americans and flown to the United States, where a grand jury tries to decide whether they should be charged with air piracy.

SC

CASE 4
A man who has been unemployed for several months is caught by the police taking things from garbage cans without the owners' permission. He is charged with criminal trespass and petty theft. He explains that many people throw away good clothing in their trash that his children could use for the winter months.

SC

CASE 5
A court has ordered that the children of a broken family should spend half the year with the father and half with the mother. The mother knows that the father likes to have wild parties with drugs and alcohol. She is afraid for the safety of her children when they are with their father. One night a friend calls and warns her of a party that is going on that very evening. She drives over to the father's house and sneaks the children out through the back door. The next morning, when the father finds the children gone, he calls the police and they arrest the mother for kidnapping.

SC

74 FAIRNESS

- Present and drill the trait information.
- Review past traits and verses, as well as the theme verse.
- Present the cases on this and the following page in the manner best suited to your class. Suggestions include: (1) Presenting one case at a time, then stopping to discuss it; (2) Dividing the class into small groups, directing them to come to a conclusion about each case; (3) Dividing the class into five groups, assigning each one a case to consider and present to the class.

SPIN-OFF

COURT IN SESSION. Using the cases from SP 74 and 75, instruct teams of students to present each case, courtroom style, to the class. You will need a judge, jury, attorneys, plaintiffs, defendants, court reporter, and bailiff. Option: Use current judicial issues in place of the cases in the book.

75 CASES, CONTINUED

- Complete page as directed.
- If students seem to enjoy this activity, ask them to create their own "caseload" for the class to consider.

Serve your students by promoting justice.

76 FRIENDLINESS: SERVANT STORY AND INTERMISSION

- Read trait information.
- Read the story and discuss.

SPIN-OFF

THE BEST FRIEND. Instruct students to write out the qualities they would demonstrate if they were "The Best Friend In the World" to their present friends.

- Intermission
  - Give time for students to consider what help Darcie might have asked them to give to Sa Joon.
  - Call on students to state their opinions.
  - Discuss together things that students wish someone would teach them. In a way that does not violate student confidences, you may wish to use some of their ideas as suggestions to parents for projects that they could do with their children.

Serve your students by reaching out to them regardless of their response.

77 SERVANT STORY AND FOLLOW-UP QUESTIONS

- Follow-up questions:

1. How did Darcie meet Sa Joon? [In the locker room, crying.]
2. What was Sa Joon's reason for crying? [Felt she had no friends.]
3. What was the first step in Darcie's attempt to make Sa Joon feel cared for? [Made arrangements for Sa Joon to come to her house for dinner.]
4. What did Darcie and her family do to help Sa Joon enjoy herself? [Brothers piled peas on their knives; whole family was there; Darcie gave her a bear to share.]
5. What had Darcie learned about having fun with people? [More fun to do things together than sit around.]
6. What people and plans did Darcie arrange to help Sa Joon feel comfortable in this country? [David taught her to use the computer; Betty taught her to cook American food; Tony taught her how to play basketball; Henry showed her how to get around on a bike.]
7. Describe Darcie's mixed feelings during this time. [She was happy and sad; sometimes jealous.]
8. What advice did Darcie receive from her mother? [It is important to make friends, but it is also important to share them.] What good advice have you received from your mother? [Student choice.]
9. What conclusion did Darcie come to after hearing the advice? [I can be greedy about my friends and lose them or be generous with them and keep them. She chose to keep them.]
10. How might the story have ended if Darcie had chosen to raise a jealous fuss? What impact would her behavior have had on Sa Joon? On her friends? On her mother? [Student choice.]

The Project Servant suggestions for this unit may be found on page 94 of this book.

FRIENDLINESS

Definition: Reaching out to others in a warm-hearted way.

Serving by Being Kind

Opposite: Responding with coolness to those around me.

Bible words:
"Perfume and incense bring joy to the heart, and the pleasantness of one's friend springs from his earnest counsel." Proverbs 27:9

SERVANT STORY

Making Friends, Sharing Friends

"Whew!" said Darcie as she wiped her wet forehead. "Mr. Parson gave us a long workout today!"

"What's new," said Monica. Darcie and Monica were on the track relay team. Mr. Parson, their coach, was getting them ready for the city's relay meet at the end of the month.

Darcie was putting her track shoes into her duffle bag when she heard the sound of crying coming from behind the gym lockers. When she poked her head around the corner, she saw Sa Joon crying into a towel.

"Sa Joon," said Darcie, "what's the matter?"

Sa Joon tried to stop her tears, but they came out anyway. Darcie patted her shoulder and wished she knew how to help. "I'll stay here with her until she's better," thought Darcie. Finally, the tears wore out and dried up.

Sa Joon had been a student at Darcie's school for only one month. She was from the country of Korea and was in America with her parents while her father was studying for one semester at the university. She spoke English, but not well enough to be easily understood. All that she said to Darcie was "no friends."

Darcie was the right person to say that to, because she was good at making friends. She coaxed Sa Joon out of the locker room. They walked together to the parking lot where Darcie's mother was waiting for her. At the car, Darcie introduced her mother to Sa Joon.

As Darcie pulled away, she was relieved to see Sa Joon wave to her. "We'll just have to make sure that 'no friends' turns to 'many friends,'" she thought.

Arrangements were made for Sa Joon to visit the Carlisle home the following Friday. At dinner, Darcie's two older brothers got the family laughing when they tried to see who could pile the most peas onto a dinner knife. Sa Joon laughed, too, and seemed glad to be there.

After dinner, the girls went into Darcie's bedroom. She had a stuffed animal collection that covered the bed and filled the shelves. Sa Joon looked at each one carefully, obviously enjoying the cloth zoo. She especially seemed to like a small snuggly bear with a heart sewn onto his chest.

"You can take him home for awhile, if you want to, Sa Joon," said Darcie, holding the bear out to her new friend. Sa Joon said, "No, no. Your bear, not mine."

Darcie tried again and said, "We'll share the bear." She moved her hand out and back as she spoke, hoping the gesture would explain the message. Sa Joon understood and shyly took the bear.

Darcie was good at having fun with friends. She had learned that it was easier to have fun with someone if you did things together. So Darcie's job became one of finding things for Sa Joon to

---

do and locating people with whom to do them. She spent the next few days doing just that.

"That's right. Now press this button to clear the screen," said David to Sa Joon. He was teaching her how to use the computer as a favor to Darcie. It turned out to be a favor to him, too, because by helping Sa Joon learn to use the computer, he came up with a program idea that would help kids learn to speak English. "I'm going to enter the program into the contest at the computer store downtown," he said after the lesson. He wasn't sure Sa Joon understood all of that, but he knew she would soon enough. At school, David and Sa Joon would look at computer books and ads in magazines. One day she left Darcie in the middle of a sentence to go look at the new office computer with David. Darcie couldn't decide whether to be sad or glad.

In the meantime, Sa Joon was also learning how to cook American food. Betty had agreed to give her four cooking lessons. The two girls had a great time in Betty's kitchen cooking hamburgers, fried chicken, tacos, and apple pie. It was so much fun that they decided to have Sa Joon teach Betty how to cook Korean food. Darcie was happy that things were going so well, but once in a while she felt left out and a little jealous.

On two Saturdays in a row, Tony taught Sa Joon how to play a basic game of basketball. "She's a natural, Darcie," he said when Darcie walked onto the outdoor court.

"Yes, I know. Coach Parson has asked her to be on the relay team for the meet next week," said Darcie.

Henry was reluctant to become friends with Sa Joon. It wasn't that he didn't like her or want to be friendly; it was that he was shy. In a moment of courage, he told Darcie that he would like to teach Sa Joon how to get around town on her bike.

"That's great, Henry," said Darcie. They talked it over with Sa Joon and set a time for their tour

on bikes. Darcie was hoping that they would invite her to go along, but they didn't think of it.

That night in her room, Darcie sat among her stuffed animals feeling lonely. Her mother came in to show her the gift she had bought for her aunt's birthday, but Darcie hardly even looked at it.

"What's up, sweetie?" asked her mother. "You look like you've lost your best friend." Her mom said that nearly every time Darcie looked sad, but this time it was true. Darcie began to cry like Sa Joon had done that day in the locker room.

Mom comforted her and listened to her tell how she had helped Sa Joon find new friends. "But now I feel like they like her better than they like me," she said.

Mom understood and said, "Darcie, I just want to say one little thing. It is important to make friends but it is also important to share them." She hugged her daughter and left the room to let Darcie think about things.

Darcie thought, "I guess that I can be greedy about my friends and lose them or be generous with them and keep them." She turned over on her bed and looked her stuffed dog in the eye. "Sounds simple enough. I choose to keep them."

The next day, Sa Joon asked Darcie to come over to her house after school. When Darcie entered the house, Sa Joon led her into the kitchen where, on the table, was a cake and a card. Sa Joon had made the cake herself, and the card had been designed and printed on the computer. The cake said, "To my friend." The card said, "Dear Darcie, You have taken me from no friends to many friends. I am happy here now. May I be your good friend forever? Love, Sa Joon."

Darcie said, "Yes, you can be my good friend forever." To herself she said, "Making friends is fun, but keeping them is more fun."

INTERMISSION

If you were one of Darcie's friends, what might she have asked you to teach Sa Joon? What do you wish someone would teach you to do?

■■ NEXT-TIME NOTES
to make next time better

SP 68: _____

SP 69: _____

SP 70: _____

SP 71: _____

SP 72: _____

SP 73: _____

SP 74: _____

SP 75: _____

SP 76: _____

SP 77: _____

PROJECT SERVANT: _____

OTHER: _____

■ AFTERTHOUGHTS
Thoughts too good to lose • Kidquotes • Thoughts from God • Ideas

_____

_____

_____

_____

_____

_____

STEP ONE

This is what God says about Hezekiah: "In everything that he undertook in the service of God's temple and in obedience to the law and the commands, he sought his God and worked wholeheartedly. And so he prospered." That is a mouthful of initiative and love.

Hezekiah found things to do and he did them for the God he loved.

Our world seems to be in the mood to "let the other guy do it. I'm busy." We need some Hezekiahs and Nehemiahs and Mordecais and Esthers to show kindness toward others as well as a spirit of initiative and love for the service of God. Wholehearted followers of Jesus Christ are in demand.

With this in mind, picture your class as a training center for future greats of the faith. Take the initiative in grooming your students to serve wholeheartedly with initiative, love, and kindness.

PATTERNING

Good took the initiative in reaching out to us. We were not capable of reaching out, or even responding to Him. Example His initiative by reaching out to your students with initiative. Come up with ways to love them wholeheartedly.

I will improve my: _____ moods, _____ listening skills, _____ encouragements, _____ creativity, _____ parent contacts, and _____ prayer habits.

CHEWABLES
Bite-sized thoughts from God's Word

Select one thought to "chew on" during this unit:

"I said to them, 'You see the trouble we are in: Jerusalem lies in ruins, and its gates have been burned with fire. Come, let us rebuild the wall of Jerusalem, and we will no longer be in disgrace.' " Nehemiah 2:17

"Then Daniel went to Arioch, whom the king had appointed to execute the men of Babylon, and said to him, 'Do not execute the wise men of Babylon. Take me to the king, and I will interpret his dream for him.' " Daniel 2:24

"Then Esther sent this reply to Mordecai: 'Go, gather together all the Jews who are in Susa, and fast for me. Do not eat or drink for three days, night or day. I and my maids will fast as you do. When this is done, I will go to the king, even though it is against the law. And if I perish, I perish.' " Esther 4:15, 16

UNIT INFORMATION

Theme Verse:
Romans 12:16
"Do not be conceited."

Esther Study:
The Jews celebrate their successful defense against Haman's decree.

PART A: INITIATIVE

Purpose:
To show, in story form, one way of taking the initiative in sharing Christ.

Approach:
Talking about Jesus can be done in a natural way. God must be pleased to hear His children telling others about His greatness.

Definition:
Carrying an idea from my mind into reality.

Opposite:
Letting others get things started.

Trait Verse:
James 1:22
"Do not merely listen to the word, and so deceive yourselves. Do what it says."

Visual Reinforcement:
Ask for volunteers to design an attractive poster using the unit's subtitle (Serving by Being Inventive) and theme verse. Display it in a conspicuous place.

Use light bulbs as a reminder of the need for good ideas. Place them on worksheets, hang them from the ceilings, or tape them to desks.

Ideas:
"Do it!" Instruct students to choose one of their helpful good ideas and do it. Discuss results of the activity.

Use as Desired:
SP 80, Proud Facts

PART B: LOVE

Purpose:
To show the priority of loving one another.

Approach:
God says that loving His children is the second greatest thing that I can do.

Definition:
Caring strongly for a person or thing.

Opposite:
Not caring about a person or thing.

Trait Verse:
I Peter 4:8
"Above all, love each other deeply, because love covers over a multitude of sins."

Visual Reinforcement:
Bring a cloth to class. Let it represent love. Use it to cover some "sins" represented by any small objects chosen by the class. Devote a period of time to investigating the idea of love covering a multitude of sins, as mentioned in the trait verse. Suggest that a person is not distracted by the sins of another when looking through the eyes of God's love. Note, however, that this does not mean we are to pretend everything and everyone is perfect. Instead, point out that when we are feeling loving toward someone, their faults do not seem as big to us.

Ideas:
Compose a "Surprised By Love" inventory sheet. Use student ideas from SP 82 naming ways Jesus showed love in unexpected ways. Post the sheet as an encouragement to all of you that Jesus loves to surprise us with His love.

Use as Desired:
SP 82, Supernatural Love

PART C: BOLDNESS

Purpose:
To stimulate students toward serving God boldly.

To provide examples of bold service.

Approach:
There are many bold servants of God.

God is ready to give me boldness and help me serve Him daringly.

Definition:
Facing life in a daring way.

Opposite:
Facing life in a cowardly way.

Trait Verse:
Psalm 138:3
"When I called, You answered me; You made me bold and stouthearted."

Visual Reinforcement:
Instruct students to design their own "stout hearts" energized by God. Display and enjoy.

Ideas:
Compile a list of descriptive words that reflect the feeling and action of bold and daring. Post for use in suggested Spin-Off for SP 83.

Present Hebrews 4:16. Compare our ability to boldly approach the throne of God with Esther's inability to boldly approach Xerxes without fear. Once again, God outshines them all!

Use as Desired:
SP 83, Bold and Daring
SP 87, Purim
TG 95, Project Servant

MY PLAN FOR THIS UNIT

_____

_____

_____

_____

78 INTRO TO UNIT

- Read through text.
- Define the words "conceited" and "humble."
  - ◆ Call on students to give you examples of a conceited person.
  - ◆ Call on other students to explain the various feelings one gets when with a conceited person.
  - ◆ Repeat with examples and responses of a humble person.
  - ◆ Ask students to give you three reasons they think God included this statement in the Bible.
- Ink in the page.
  - ◆ As students ink in the page, discuss the following:
1. Name several reasons Jesus could have acted in a proud and conceited manner. What kept Him from acting conceited? How are conceit and confidence different?
2. Before Paul met Jesus, he was proud and conceited about his background. Listen, then be prepared to suggest ways that Paul, then Saul, would have lived if he were alive today and had not yet met Jesus.

"If anyone else thinks he has reasons to put confidence in the flesh, I have more: circumcised on the eighth day, of the people of Israel, of the tribe of Benjamin, a Hebrew of Hebrews; in regard to the law, a Pharisee; as for zeal, persecuting the church; as for legalistic righteousness, faultless" (Philippians 3:4-6).

3. After Paul met Jesus, He changed from a conceited Pharisee to a humble follower. Listen, then be prepared to suggest the kinds of activities Paul might be involved in if he were alive today.

"Five times I received from the Jews the forty lashes minus one. Three times I was beaten with rods, once I was stoned, three times I was shipwrecked, I spent a night and a day in the open sea, I have been constantly on the move. I have been in danger from rivers, in danger from bandits, in danger from my own countrymen, in danger from Gentiles; in danger in the city, in danger in the country, in danger at sea; and in danger from false brothers. I have labored and toiled and have often gone without sleep; I have known hunger and thirst and have often gone without food; I have been cold and naked. Besides everything else, I face daily the pressure of my concern for all the churches . . . If I must boast, I will boast of the things that show my weakness. The God and Father of the Lord Jesus, who is to be praised forever, knows that I am not lying" (2 Corinthians 11:24-31).

4. Name some reasons Christians could use as an excuse for being conceited. [Examples: Secure future in Heaven; friends with the God of the universe; help always available from our Heavenly Father.] Which of these three qualities would keep a child of God from being conceited? Why?
a. Thankfulness
b. Love for God and others
c. Wisdom

79 INITIATIVE: SERVANT STORY AND INTERMISSION

- Read trait information.
  - ◆ Review past traits and verses.
- Read and discuss the story.

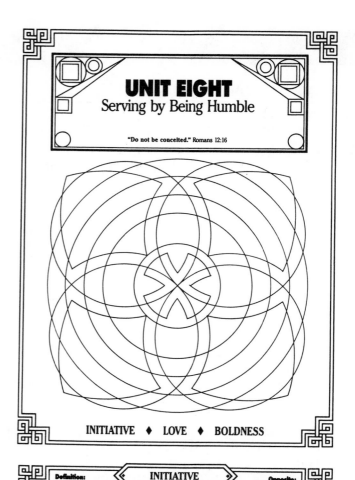

UNIT EIGHT
Serving by Being Humble

"Do not be conceited." Romans 12:16

INITIATIVE ◆ LOVE ◆ BOLDNESS

Definition:
Carrying an idea from my mind into reality.

INITIATIVE
Serving by Being Inventive

Opposite:
Letting others get things started.

Bible words:
"Do not merely listen to the word, and so deceive yourselves. Do what it says." James 1:22

Friends Forever

On their next bike ride, Sa Joon, or "Saj" as the group liked to call her, invited Henry to go with her family to the zoo the following Sunday.

"Thanks, but I go to church on Sundays," he said.

"Oh, yes, I forgot," she said. "I've never been to church."

"Never?" asked Henry.

"Not really, just to . . . what you call them . . . uh . . . funerals," she said. "What is so good about church, Henry?"

"It's that I go there to worship God, the One who made the universe and everything in it," he said.

"I see." She sped ahead of him. "Well, sorry you can't go to the zoo." She had reached her turn-off and was waving goodbye to Henry. He waved back.

The next day at school, while Henry was shooting hoops with Tony, he mentioned his talk with Saj about church. "You mean she's not a Christian?" asked Tony. "Why is she going to a Christian school, then?"

Henry laughed. "Come on, Bounce, you know that everybody who goes to this school isn't a Christian." Tony liked it when people called him by his nickname.

"Yeah, I guess you're right," said Tony.

When Betty and Darcie heard that Saj had never been to church, they said, "So Henry, why don't you invite her to your church?"

"Well, I thought about it, but I wasn't sure she would want to go," he said.

"It doesn't matter if she goes with you," said David. "What matters is that you invited her."

The next time Henry saw Saj, he said, "I was wondering if you would like to come to church with me some Sunday."

"I don't know. I'll have to think about it," she said. Henry's heart was beating quickly. It wasn't used to his boldness.

At lunch, David said, "Why are you making such a big deal about talking to someone about God?" The group could feel one of David's logical speeches coming on. "After all, God is the most powerful Being in the universe, and He loves us. Why **not** talk about Him? We talk about our parents and our friends and our vacation plans to people, so why not talk about God in the same way? I just don't get it." David had a way of explaining things so that people could understand them.

Betty said, "I think David's right, and I want to try talking about God in the same way I talk about other things. I'm going to start doing that today."

"Me, too," said Darcie. David and Henry joined in, too. Tony was quiet, and he left the lunch table early.

On the bus ride home, Betty sat next to Sandra, a fifth grader. They saw a rainbow in the sky and Betty said, "Just think! We are loved by the God who makes those."

After school, Darcie carried two grocery bags home from the store for her neighbor, Mrs. Werlie. The lady was so glad for the help that she gave Darcie a pint of strawberry freezer jam she had made that morning. Darcie thanked her and said, "Isn't it nice of God to make strawberries?" Mrs. Werlie agreed.

CONTINUED

David spoke of God to the mailman. He had gotten some letters mixed up and needed to make a special trip back to David's block. "I'm not having such a good day," he said.

"That's too bad," said David. "At least it's good to know that God loves you."

The next day each person reported to the others. They were excited. "This is great," said Betty. "What did you do, Tony?" she asked. Tony just shook his head and looked away.

A few days later, the group and Saj were eating apples under the tree in Darcie's yard. "These are so good," said Betty.

"Yes. Who would ever guess that they were the cause of such trouble," said Darcie.

"What trouble," asked Saj.

"They weren't the **cause** of any trouble," said David. "They were part of the problem. And no one knows for sure that it was an apple that they ate, Darcie."

Saj looked confused and asked, "**What** are you talking about?" The group let David explain.

"Well, when God created Adam and Eve, the world was a perfect place. God would walk with them in their garden home. They would live forever as long as they didn't eat the fruit of one certain tree."

"What tree was that? And why couldn't they eat from it," asked Saj.

"The fruit of this tree was more than just tasty; it was powerful. With a single swallow, they would be given the ability to do right **and** wrong. Once they could do wrong, or sin, their life in the garden and their friendship with God would end."

"And," said Darcie, "the sin would pass on to their children and their children's children until it reached everyone who would ever be born."

"Except One," said Henry.

"Anyway," said David, eager to get to the good part of the story, "it was God's enemy, Satan, who got them to disobey God and eat the fruit. He wanted to spoil God's plan for man because He hates God and wants to be in charge."

"One of God's rules is that when sin is committed, someone's blood must be shed. He loved Adam and Eve yet He had to obey His own rule. So, he killed two lambs in their place."

"Then, one day, God came to earth Himself wearing the body of a person. His name was Jesus, and He chose to die in our place, just like those little lambs."

"He did?" asked Saj. "Your God did that?"

Henry shook his head and said, "Yes, He did. And then He came back to life and returned to Heaven. He's there now getting it ready for anyone who believes that He died in their place."

"He's saving a spot for me," said Darcie.

"Me, too," said David.

"Me, three," said Betty.

"Me, four," said Henry.

Tony said, "Not me." Everyone stared at him in unbelief. "But I'd like Him to save me a place."

"Me, too," said Saj.

And there, under the apple tree, two more reservations were made for Heaven. "Now we're **really** forever friends," said Darcie.

INTER**MISSION**

David explained God's plan of salvation in the way he liked best. If you had been under the apple tree that day, how would you have explained it? Write your ideas on a separate piece of paper.

Definition:		Opposite:
Caring strongly for a person or thing.	**LOVE**	Not caring about a person or thing.
	Serving by Being Unselfish	

Bible words:
"Above all, love each other deeply, because love covers over a multitude of sins." I Peter 4:8

COMMAND CENTER

God is eager for His family to love each other deeply. In fact, of all the things He tells us to do for one another, loving each other is tops.
Select six verses from the pool of verses at the bottom of the page. Fit them into the command center in the order you believe they belong.

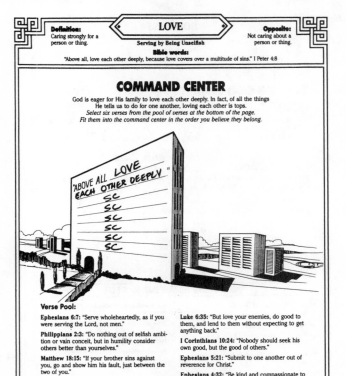

Verse Pool:

Ephesians 6:7: "Serve wholeheartedly, as if you were serving the Lord, not men."

Philippians 2:3: "Do nothing out of selfish ambition or vain conceit, but in humility consider others better than yourselves."

Matthew 18:15: "If your brother sins against you, go and show him his fault, just between the two of you."

Ephesians 5:19: "Speak to one another with psalms, hymns and spiritual songs."

Luke 6:35: "But love your enemies, do good to them, and lend to them without expecting to get anything back."

I Corinthians 10:24: "Nobody should seek his own good, but the good of others."

Ephesians 5:21: "Submit to one another out of reverence for Christ."

Ephesians 4:32: "Be kind and compassionate to one another, forgiving each other, just as in Christ God forgave you."

80 STORY, CONTINUED, AND FOLLOW-UP QUESTIONS

● Follow-up questions:

1. What two nicknames are mentioned in this story? ["Saj" for Sa Joon and "Bounce" for Tony.]

2. What was Henry hoping to do? [Invite Sa Joon to church.]

3. Why does Henry like to go to church? [To worship God.] What do you think he does to show his worship of God? [Student choice.]

4. What logical facts did David give for talking to people about God? [God is the most powerful Being in the universe; He loves us; we talk about other things easily.]

5. What did Betty, Darcie, and David do and say that same day? [Betty talked to Sandra about God making a rainbow; Darcie helped her neighbor and commented on God's kindness in making strawberries; David mentioned to the mailman that God loved him.]

6. When the friends were in Darcie's yard, what prompted the discussion about sin and trusting Jesus? [Eating apples under a tree.]

7. What surprise did Tony give the group? [He had never trusted Jesus as His Savior.]

8. What kinds of feelings do you think Tony had been feeling during this story? [Student choice.]

9. Henry's efforts to tell Sa Joon about Jesus paid off. Consider how his efforts might spread across the ocean. [Sa Joon could go back to Korea and tell her friends about Jesus.]

10. How might this story have been different if Henry and the others had not used their initiative to be bold in their talk about God? [Student choice.]

*Serve your students by using **your** good ideas.*

 SPIN-OFF

PROUD FACTS. Direct each student to think of one fact about God that he/she would want others to know. The student then designs a way of communicating the proud fact, i.e., conversation, cartoon, skit, drawing, poem, song. This will be a helpful exercise in preparing your class for the unit's Project Servant activity.

81 LOVE

● Read trait information.

● Review past traits and verses, including theme verse.

● Command Center

◆ Allow time for students to read the verses, rank them, then enter them into the Command Center.

◆ Stress the importance of following one's own opinions when ranking the commands. Discuss results.

◆ Ask students to write one name on each level as an example of a person who seems to demonstrate the truth of the verse. Call on some students to explain their choices.

Serve your students with the supernatural love of Jesus.

82 LOVING WITH THE LOVE OF JESUS

- Read upper page and discuss the difference between "natural" and "supernatural."
- The Supernatural Love of Jesus
  - ◗ Give instructions and accept questions about the activity.
  - ◗ Students are to weigh the situation, then select a response to it that would be supernatural, rather than natural. Example for #1: David would control his anger, forgive Michael, then teach him how to avoid erasing diskettes in the future.
  - ◗ Call on students to read their supernatural ideas to the class.
  - ◗ Challenge students to let God's love rule their choices.
- Seek to convey the truth that we cannot manufacture supernatural love. It must come from God, then flow through us to others.
  - ◗ Briefly discuss the "blocks" that hinder His flow of love.

 SPIN-OFF

SUPERNATURAL LOVE. Dramatize, illustrate, or poetically present some student examples of supernatural love from SP 82. Present the completed assignments to another class.

---

83 BOLDNESS

- Read and discuss trait information.
- Review past traits and verses.
- Serving God Boldly
  - ◗ Complete page as directed.
  - ◗ Review the events in David's life, noting that these are just a few of the many exciting things he did.
  - ◗ Spark interest in the idea of one day talking to David in Heaven about his bold and daring life on earth.

 SPIN-OFF

BOLD AND DARING. Assign students a creative writing project which requires them to write a story about a fictional servant of God who lives today and serves with boldness as King David did.

Serve your students by being a daring manager of children who boldly strives for excellence as an educator.

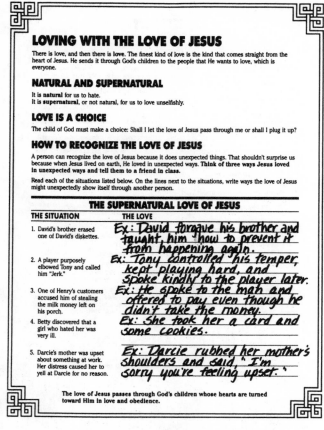

LOVING WITH THE LOVE OF JESUS

There is love, and then there is love. The finest kind of love is the kind that comes straight from the heart of Jesus. He sends it through God's children to the people that He wants to love, which is everyone.

NATURAL AND SUPERNATURAL

It is natural for us to hate.
It is supernatural, or not natural, for us to love unselfishly.

LOVE IS A CHOICE

The child of God must make a choice: Shall I let the love of Jesus pass through me or shall I plug it up?

HOW TO RECOGNIZE THE LOVE OF JESUS

A person can recognize the love of Jesus because it does unexpected things. That shouldn't surprise us because when Jesus lived on earth, He loved in unexpected ways. Think of three ways Jesus loved in unexpected ways and tell them to a friend in class.

Read each of the situations listed below. On the lines next to the situations, write ways the love of Jesus might unexpectedly show itself through another person.

THE SUPERNATURAL LOVE OF JESUS

THE SITUATION	THE LOVE
1. David's brother erased one of David's diskettes.	*Ex: David forgave his brother and taught him how to prevent it from happening again.*
2. A player purposely elbowed Tony and called him "Jerk."	*Ex: Tony controlled his temper, kept playing hard, and spoke kindly to the player later.*
3. One of Henry's customers accused him of stealing the milk money left on his porch.	*Ex: He spoke to the man and offered to pay even though he didn't take the money.*
4. Betty discovered that a girl who hated her was very ill.	*Ex: She took her a card and some cookies.*
5. Darcie's mother was upset about something at work. Her distress caused her to yell at Darcie for no reason.	*Ex: Darcie rubbed her mother's shoulders and said, "I'm sorry you're feeling upset."*

The love of Jesus passes through God's children whose hearts are turned toward Him in love and obedience.

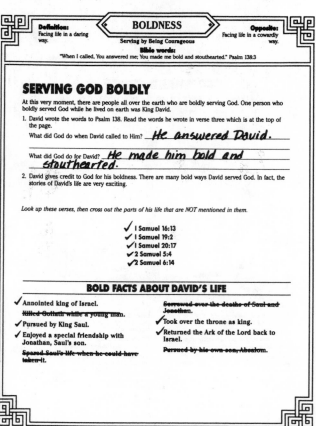

Definition: Facing life in a daring way.	◄ BOLDNESS ► Serving by Being Courageous	Opposite: Facing life in a cowardly way.

Bible words:
"When I called, You answered me; You made me bold and stouthearted." Psalm 138:3

SERVING GOD BOLDLY

At this very moment, there are people all over the earth who are boldly serving God. One person who boldly served God while he lived on earth was King David.

1. David wrote the words to Psalm 138. Read the words he wrote in verse three which is at the top of the page.

What did God do when David called to Him? *He answered David.*

What did God do for David? *He made him bold and stouthearted.*

2. David gives credit to God for his boldness. There are many bold ways David served God. In fact, the stories of David's life are very exciting.

Look up these verses, then cross out the parts of his life that are NOT mentioned in them.

✓ I Samuel 16:13
✓ I Samuel 19:2
✓ I Samuel 20:17
✓ 2 Samuel 5:4
✓ 2 Samuel 6:14

BOLD FACTS ABOUT DAVID'S LIFE

✓ Anointed king of Israel.
~~Killed Goliath while a young man.~~
✓ Pursued by King Saul.
✓ Enjoyed a special friendship with Jonathan, Saul's son.
~~Spared Saul's life when he could have taken it.~~
~~Sorrowed over the deaths of Saul and Jonathan.~~
✓ Took over the throne as king.
✓ Returned the Ark of the Lord back to Israel.
~~Pursued by his own son, Absalom.~~

From magazines and newspapers, select pictures of people serving one another with boldness. A picture of a fireman fighting a fire, for example, would show boldness.

Follow your teacher's instructions about collecting and mounting the pictures on this page.

LIVING BOLDLY

Student collage.

Esther and Mordecai celebrate God's deliverance.

84 LIVING BOLDLY

- Read opening paragraph together.
- Instruct students to:
  1. Look through the magazines you have provided for them.
  2. Select and cut out pictures of people boldly serving others. OR select pictures to be photocopied by a designated student.
  3. Mount the pictures in an attractive way on this page.
  4. Design borders, word balloons, or any other kinds of decorations you desire.

NOTE: Types of magazines that would be especially helpful for this activity would be "Life," "The Saturday Evening Post," "National Geographic," and trade and mission magazines. If you choose to photocopy pictures rather than cut them out, instruct students to mark the page with a paper clip and their name. Designate one or two students to take the magazines to the copy machine on behalf of the whole class.

- Take time to admire one another's efforts.
- Help students imagine being pictured in a magazine because of their bold service for God.

85 ESTHER ILLUSTRATION

- Study the picture.
  - Note the emotions of the scene.
  - Call on students to suggest possible comments being made by Esther and Mordecai in this scene.

Whatever God gives you to do,
do it as well as you can.
This is the best possible preparation
for what He may want you to do next.

86 BACKFIRE: Episode Eight Of the Esther Story

- Review past episodes.
- Read story together or individually.
- Search together for demonstrations of initiative, love, and boldness in the entire story of Esther.

ESTHER

EPISODE EIGHT

Following Haman's hanging, Esther told the curious king all of the details surrounding Haman's terrible plot. She explained that she and Mordecai were cousins and that she, too, was a Jew. The story stirred the king.

Esther fell weeping at his feet. She begged the king to show mercy to her people. He held out his golden scepter, giving her permission to stand and discuss the matter.

"If it pleases the king, make a second decree overruling the one Haman wrote," she cried. "I can't bear to see disaster fall on my people."

"Write another decree in any way you wish," said the king, "and seal it with this." He handed his ring to Mordecai, the same ring that had been on Haman's hand earlier in the day.

Once outside the king's court, Esther and Mordecai grabbed one another in a joy-filled hug. They had difficulty finding words to express their happiness over what God was doing through them.

Esther and Mordecai wasted no time in calling for the secretaries. Because a decree signed with the king's ring could not be reversed, the two cousins had to come up with a way of working around the first one. Their wise plan was this: they would grant permission from the king for all Jews to defend themselves from their enemies on the thirteenth of Adar.

The secretaries wrote out the decree in the language of every province. The news was delivered by messengers on galloping palace horses and was posted in public places by province officials. The cries of happy Jews blended into one giant shout of praise to their God.

Once the decree was written, Mordecai left the palace. He had discarded his mourning clothes and was now wearing glorious garments of blue and purple. On his head was a royal crown, and his hand displayed the king's own ring.

Word spread quickly among those who were not Jews. They became afraid, and many became Jews because they were afraid not to be. The God of the Jews did

awesome things, and they didn't want to be caught on the side of His enemies.

As the months passed, the Jews – and those who planned to kill them – prepared for the attack. All of the officials in the provinces had turned to the side of the Jews. They were afraid of Mordecai because they knew that God was on his side. Mordecai's power increased every day.

Finally, the thirteenth of Adar arrived. Haman's loyal troops began their attack but were soundly slaughtered by the Jews. Haman's ten sons were also killed. At the end of the day, the king brought the battle report to Esther and asked her if there was any other wish she wanted granted.

"If it pleases the king, give the Jews in Susa one more day to continue the battle, and let us hang Haman's ten sons from poles in the city." The king commanded that this be done. So, the Jews in Susa completed their defense in two days. Those living in the country did the job in one. Everyone stopped to celebrate on the following day. They gave gifts to one another and rejoiced in their God.

Mordecai sent letters to all of them asking them to set aside the fourteenth and fifteenth of Adar every year for a holiday. "Stop what you are doing to celebrate this day as the time when the Jews got relief from their enemies," he wrote. "Remember that on this day our sorrow was turned to joy and our mourning was changed to celebration." He then instructed them to give gifts to the poor as part of their activities. He named this holiday "Purim," because Haman had cast lots, or "pur," to choose the day of the slaughter.

Following the battles and the celebrations, things in the palace settled back into a royal pace. Xerxes remained an easy-going king. Esther continued to serve Xerxes as king and her God as Lord. Mordecai took over Haman's position as second in command. He was well-loved by the people because he cared about them and found ways of working for their good.

And so ends the story of history's loudest backfire.

---

87 BACK TO BACKFIRE

- Complete follow-up activities.
- Discuss answers.

 SPIN-OFF

PURIM. Acquaint students with the celebration of Purim by instructing them to investigate past and current traditions. Report discoveries through the written and spoken word, by illustration, and/or by demonstration.

BACKFIRE 8

1. How did the king show mercy to Esther after she fell weeping at his feet?

He granted her permission to stand and talk about the matter.

2. How did Mordecai and Esther display initiative in solving the problem of the original decree?

They gained permission to write a second decree.

3. Describe the sequence of events leading up to the Jews' victory over their enemies in Susa and in the countryside.

The Jews were able to defend themselves; Haman was hanged from his gallows.

4. What did Mordecai tell the Jews to do to express their joy over their victory and their love for God?

Stop and celebrate each year; give gifts to one another and the needy.

5. Think of the relationships described at the end of the story between Esther, King Xerxes, Mordecai, and the Lord. A diagram of our own government in America might look like this:

PRESIDENT
↓
VICE-PRESIDENT
↓
CONGRESS
↓
THE PEOPLE

Draw a similar chart showing what the government of King Xerxes might look like (be sure to include Esther, the king, Mordecai, and God). Compare your finished diagram with others in the class. In what position did you put God?

The Project Servant suggestions for this unit may be found on page 95 of this book.

◪ NEXT-TIME NOTES
to make next time better

SP 78:

SP 79:

SP 80:

SP 81:

SP 82:

SP 83:

SP 84:

SP 85:

SP 86:

SP 87:

PROJECT SERVANT:

OTHER:

♋ AFTERTHOUGHTS
Thoughts too good to lose • Kidquotes • Thoughts from God • Ideas

STEP ONE

Teachers are usually ready for school to end, but what seems to catch them off guard is the work, the frustration of the undone, and the goodbyes.

The urgency we feel in wanting to be sure our students are prepared to move on to the next grade reminds me of Jesus' mood before He said goodbye to His friends. He talked to them about things to come and repeated important truths to make sure they understood. Following this, He did what many of us do: He talked to His Father about them in prayer. His is recorded in John 17. Following His example, let us pray this prayer for our students:

Father, my time with these children is nearly over. I love them and I will miss them. I pray that they will grow toward You and receive salvation through Your Son, Jesus Christ.

I have, through Your strength, done the work that You have given me to do. They have learned of Your love for them, of Your plan of redemption, and of Your interest in their lives. They have learned that You are trustworthy and kind, and that You possess power. Please take this knowledge and seal it within them.

I pray that they may know the joy of Your Spirit as they walk with You. I pray that You will protect them from this evil day and from the corruption that is around them.

Please keep them exposed to Your Word and open to it. I pray for their families, that they, too, will know You as their God and Friend.

Father, let me worship You with them in Heaven one day. Finally, Father, please let them grow in Your love and let the overflow reach those around them.

I pray all of this in the name of Your Son, Jesus Christ, whose obedience and love for You have set us free.
Amen.

PATTERNING

God did not leave the disciples without evidence of His Son's life on earth. He sent them – and us – the Gift of His Spirit. Follow this example, and leave your students with a memory of you and your love for them. A simple card, bookmark, printed prayer, or picture will tangibly remind them in years to come that you – and your God – cared for and loved them.

CHEWABLES
Bite-sized thoughts from God's Word

Select one thought to "chew on" during this unit:

"It was just before the Passover Feast. Jesus knew that the time had come for Him to leave this world and go to the Father. Having loved His own who were in the world, He now showed them the full extent of His love." John 13:1

"For the Lamb at the center of the throne will be their shepherd; He will lead them to springs of living water. And God will wipe away every tear from their eyes." Revelation 7:17

"I know that You can do all things; no plan of Yours can be thwarted." Job 42:2

NOTE: Because this unit is a general review of the book, some usual features of the SPECIFICS page will not apply.

UNIT INFORMATION

Theme Verse:
Romans 12:13-16
"Share with God's people who are in need. Practice hospitality. Bless those who persecute you; bless and do not curse. Rejoice with those who rejoice; mourn with those who mourn. Live in harmony with one another. Do not be proud, but be willing to associate with people of low position. Do not be conceited."

Esther Study:
Personal response.

Purpose:
To review and evaluate what has been learned in this book.

Approach:
What I have learned can help me become the servant I want to be.

Definition:
N/A

Opposite:
N/A

Trait Verse:
N/A

Visual Reinforcement:
Call upon the skills of a calligrapher to write out the theme verse, titling it "Living to Serve." Photocopy the printed verse onto 4" x 6" cards. On the back of the card, attach a snapshot you have taken of your class. Date and sign it. Present it as a gift to your students at a time of your choice.

Ideas:
Following completion of the Gameboard Review on SP 94, collect the questions students wrote in the blanks on their gameboards. Divide the class into teams and compete to see which team can answer the most questions perfectly. Answers may be written or given orally.

Use as Desired:
SP 92, What Do You Think?

MY PLAN FOR THIS UNIT

_____

_____

_____

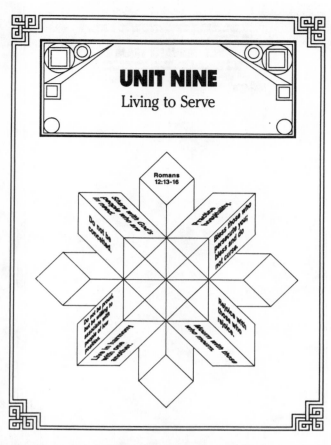

UNIT NINE
Living to Serve

Romans
12:13-16

Share with God's
people who are
in need.

Practice
hospitality.

Bless those who
persecute you;
bless and do
not curse.

Do not be
conceited.

Rejoice with
those with
who rejoice.

Mourn with those
who mourn.

SUMMER PLANS

When it came time for school to end, the group had mixed feelings. Before school had started in September, they hardly knew each other. Now they were best friends.

What began as a way to help one person, ended as help to lots of people. "This servant stuff is okay," said Tony. "Of course, that's because it's the Jesus way of living." Tony was enjoying being a child of God.

They agreed to send and receive messages at the little grocery store near the school. Mr. Friesen, the store owner, agreed to let them keep a clipboard at the register for messages.

1. At the end of summer, what do you think the clipboard looked like? Write your idea on a separate sheet of paper.

2. What do you think each member of the group did during the summer?
   David: SC
   Darcie: SC
   Tony: SC
   Betty: SC
   Henry: SC

3. If David were asked what the group learned about serving others this year, what do you think he would say?
   SC

4. Using your memory, recall ways that each member of the group served in the stories.
   Tony _____
   Darcie _____
   David _____
   Betty _____
   Henry _____
   Your Name _____

5. Write your name on the last line of the list. Recall ways that you served others this year.

88 INTRO TO UNIT

● Read through the text together.
   ◗ Call on students to recite the entire verse package.
● Ink in the page.
   ◗ As students ink in the page, discuss what students believe Jesus meant by following Him.
   ◗ Ask them to describe a servant who really serves like Jesus.
   ◗ Close in prayer, asking God to cause you and your students to serve Him daringly.

UNIT NINE, PART ONE: MIND MARATHON

The following activity is one part of three designed to help students serve their classmates by helping them recall concepts presented during the year. Parts Two and Three are located on pages 84 and 85, respectively.

Our lives are full of acronyms. NASA stands for the National Aeronautics and Space Administration. RAM stands for random access memory. GE is short for General Electric. Working individually or in teams, create acronyms for all the concepts you have worked with this year. You might want to set up a panel of judges to pick the most meaningful creations and award prizes. Those with an artistic streak could produce some attractive banners to hang in the classroom.

Here is an example to get you started:
L lending
O ourselves
V very
E easily

89 SERVANT STORY

● Read and complete the page together, enjoying the memories and conversation it produces.
● Ask these questions to quiz your students on how well they really know the servant team:
   1. Who has a dog named Jerome? [Henry]
   2. Whose family has the most money? [Betty's]
   3. To whom would you go with a math problem? [David]
   4. In whose home would you be the most crowded? [Henry's]
   5. Who could be described as bubbly? [Darcie]
   6. Whose mother was killed in a car accident? [Tony's]

CONTINUED

- Follow-up questions:
  CONTINUED

  7. Who seems to care almost too much about what people think? [Betty]
  8. Who collects stuffed animals? [Darcie]
  9. Who has a best friend named Travis? [Tony]
  10. Who seems to have the most difficulty understanding people? [David]
- A By-The-Way Fact: David did win the computer programming contest and received his own computer, monitor, and screen.

90 THE SERVANT TEAM

Prior to this activity, collect catalogs or other magazines with pictures of children in them.
- Read the instructions together.
- Complete the activity.
  ♦ Take time to compare impressions your students have built about the members of the servant team.

91 ESTHER ILLUSTRATION

- Study the collage.
  ♦ Discuss the events it represents.
  ♦ Call on students to tell the class the parts of the story they most enjoyed.

UNIT NINE, PART TWO: MIND MARATHON

Divide the class into a few small groups. Each group has the challenging assignment of choosing a famous person in history who best displayed one or more of this year's concepts in word or deed. The group must then prepare a short play about this person. After the performance, the rest of the class must try to guess who the person was. The performing group should then explain the reasons for their choice and allow comments and questions from the audience.

Look through magazines and catalogs until you find five pictures of people whom you think most closely match your idea of the kids on the servant team. Label each picture.

THE SERVANT TEAM
Tony "Bounce" Erving ★ David "Doc" Peterson ★ Elizabeth "Betty" Canterbury
Darcie Carlisle ★ Henry "Klink" Klinkdale (and Jerome!)

Thinking back on Backfire!

THINKING BACK ON BACKFIRE

You have been reading about Esther for several months. Now it is your turn to put some of your thoughts on paper!

1. What could a person learn about God from the story of Esther?
   SL _____

2. What could a person learn about serving God from the story of Esther?
   SL _____

   About serving others? _____

3. Describe in complete sentences the sights and sounds you might have seen and heard if you had been:

   a. The horse upon which Mordecai rode the day Haman led him through the streets with full honors.
   SL _____

   b. A secretary in a meeting with Persian officials the day they received word of the king's second decree granting the Jews permission to defend themselves against the slaughter. _____
   SL _____

   c. The palace kitten on Esther's lounge chair the moment she exposed Haman's plot. _____
   SL _____

   d. A Jewish child whose mother had just received the news of Haman's plan to kill all of your people, including you. _____
   SL _____

THE KIND OF SERVANT I WANT TO BE

Use these lines to deposit your thoughts about the kind of servant you would like to be to God and others. (1) Name specific acts of service you dream of performing; (2) List two or three reasons you want to do them; (3) Write a paragraph as if someone were writing about you and your life ten years from now.

MY DREAMS OF SERVICE
SL _____
_____
_____
_____
_____
_____

REASONS I WANT TO SERVE IN THESE WAYS
SL _____
_____
_____
_____

THE LIFE AND SERVICE OF _____ **IN 19** ____
SL _____
_____
_____
_____
_____

---

92 THINKING BACK ON BACKFIRE

- Complete the page as directed.
  - ◗ Share answers and insights.
  - ◗ Discuss and reminisce as desired.

▣ SPIN-OFF

WHAT DO YOIU THINK? Some believe that the name of God is omitted from the story of Esther to keep from being irreverent to Him during Purim when the story is read as a melodrama. Ask students their opinions. Could there be another explanation?

---

93 THE KIND OF SERVANT I WANT TO BE

- Allow time for students to thoughtfully complete this page.
  - ◗ Be sensitive to their desire for privacy as they write these personal thoughts.
  - ◗ Carefully solicit volunteers to share parts of their page with the class.
  - ◗ Encourage students to share their dreams of service with a friend.
- Challenge students to ask God to fulfill their dreams of service, or others that are equally bold and daring.
  - ◗ Lead your class in a time of prayer, asking students to join you in praying out loud for one another and avenues of service.

UNIT NINE, PART THREE: MIND MARATHON

Students will create some puzzles to challenge their classmates. They could be crosswords, word searches, word jumbles, or other types. Their raw material should be the many concepts, traits, character qualities, life facts, or character names they have run across this year. Be creative! Be tricky! Be a puzzler!

94 SERVANT GAMEBOARD

- Introduce the gameboard to the class.
- Explain carefully before beginning.
  - ◗ Divide students into small groups.
  - ◗ Provide a die or a numbered game spinner for each group.
  - ◗ Each student may use a token such as a coin to mark his/her progress along the game path.
  - ◗ Students take turns moving along their gameboards, making bonus moves as they correctly answer the questions in the spaces they land on. Limit students to one bonus move per turn.
  - ◗ When landing on a space with a large question mark, students may write in their own questions on the gameboard.
- This is meant to be an orderly, but casual, exercise.
  - ◗ Participate by circulating, quizzing, and listening to answers.

95 GAMEBOARD, CONTINUED

- Continue playing.
- See "Ideas" on TG 82 for instructions in using the student-designed questions from the gameboard.

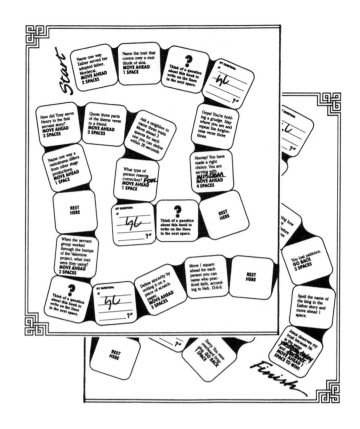

96 POSTER

- Study the picture and discuss as desired.
- Ink in the picture.
  - ◗ As students complete the page, generate discussion by thumbing through the book, randomly reviewing concepts, stories, and activities.
  - ◗ Call on students to recall facts and share impressions.

And Jesus said,
"LET THE CHILDREN COME TO ME."
Bless you, teacher, for being like Him.

◼ NEXT-TIME NOTES
to make next time better

SP 88: _____

SP 89: _____

SP 90: _____

SP 91: _____

SP 92: _____

SP 93: _____

SP 94: _____

SP 95: _____

SP 96: _____

SP 97: _____

PROJECT SERVANT: _____

OTHER: _____

AFTERTHOUGHTS
Thoughts too good to lose • Kidquotes • Thoughts from God • Ideas

_____

_____

_____

_____

_____

PROJECT SERVANT

UNIT ONE: TEACHER/STAFF APPRECIATION WEEK

Launch a teacher and staff appreciation month as a spin-off of the Project Servant Story. With your class, plan ways to focus on and praise members of the faculty and staff.

Here are some ideas to help get the project rolling:

- Rotate a revolving paper spotlight similar to the one in Fig. A. Attach the spotlight to the office door or window of the person being honored.
- Find out each teacher's favorite snack food and see that they receive it sometime during the week with a note of thanks.
- Wash the car of each teacher.
- Design buttons to give to the teachers that say things like "Peach of a Teach."
- Highlight the responsibilities of each position honored by naming them over announcements or through the school newsletter or newspaper.

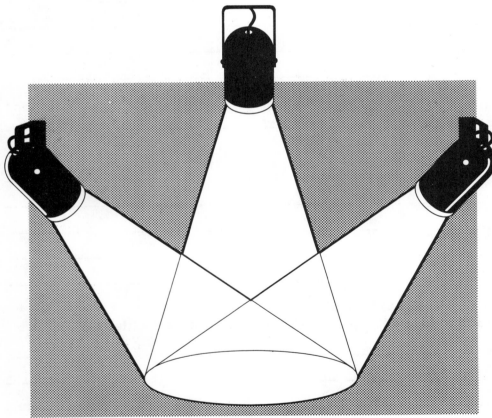

FIGURE A

FIGURE B

UNIT TWO: CONFIDENCE THROUGH NEW CHALLENGES

Plan a set of challenges that students can face several times during the unit. Provide a setting that is conducive to helping one another. Use the suggestions listed below or gather your own. Stress that this is not a competition. It is an opportunity for the group to work together to accomplish a set of goals.

If you wish, provide students with a small "personal best" record book to keep track of progress.

CHALLENGE #1: WALKING THE PIPE
Students walk blindfolded across a heavy pipe which has been placed on the ground or floor. Initially, most will need help. As time goes on, less help should be needed.

CHALLENGE #2: TIMED COMBINATIONS
Students seek to give the most answers possible within a one-minute period of time to combinations given orally by the teacher. Rotate the combinations. Again, stress the idea of "personal best" rather than "group best."

CHALLENGE #3: YO-YO TRICK
Ask students to bring yo-yos to class. Call on the help of someone who is proficient at yo-yoing to instruct students in one or two tricks.

CHALLENGE #4: JUMP ROPING
Timed jump roping as well as trick jump roping would be effective challenges. Choose the one that is most reasonable for you.

CHALLENGE #5: DROP THE COIN IN THE GLASS
Another blindfold activity, students seek to drop a coin in a glass while blindfolded, initially to the instructions of other students.

UNIT THREE: SERVING YOUNG CHILDREN

In the servant story, David led the group in finding ways to serve young children. Encourage your class to do the same by asking them to come up with ways to serve children around them.

You may wish to speak to the kindergarten and lower elementary teachers in your school to determine needs or desires they may have that could be met by sixth graders.

The following suggestions are presented only as back-up ideas in case you need them:

1. Divide your class into pairs. Each pair designs a simple, but colorful, book for preschoolers about colors, shapes, numbers, or letters.

2. Video each episode of the Esther story.

3. Make a cassette of sounds for young children to identify.

4. Share recess time, assigning recess leaders the responsibility of leading games with the young children.

5. Select two or three activities to teach to the children. For example, the class may delegate an artistic student to teach one period of finger painting. Another student might teach the children a simple "magic" trick, and so on.

6. Choose a book and have a student read to the children.

PROJECT SERVANT

UNIT FOUR: SERVING SENIOR CITIZENS

Caring service by children toward the elderly is a growing trend. However, there is nothing trendy about it. It is a real and necessary part of caring for one another.

Lead your students in a meeting which considers the variety of ways children can reach out to senior adults. Encourage them to think of wild ideas, then help them trim the wild ideas to become workable ones.

The following suggestions may be of help to you in generating ideas of your own. They are meant to be used as follow-up activities to a personal visit by the class.

1. Together In Spirit. Using as many containers as there are senior adults, students plant two bulbs in each container. A note is attached to each bulb that (1) gives care instructions, (2) introduces the student giving the gift, and (3) explains that the bulbs represent "together in spirit" and are a visual sign of a promise to return in the spring for another visit.

2. Keeping Tabs. Keep tabs on one another by asking students to select several pieces of class work to send to their elderly "partner" each month. Seek to have the seniors "report" on their activities in a similar way. This could become an incentive for both age groups to work toward specific improvement and accomplishment of goals.

3. Snapping Up Love. Assign a student as class photographer. Each month, or term, take a snapshot of each student. Make the snapshots lively, with the student in the midst of an activity, or standing holding a message of some kind for their elderly friend. If desired, line up a similar photographer at the senior center (if you are choosing to link up with one), or send your class photographer "on assignment" to take the pictures of the elderly to be given to your students.

UNIT FIVE: HONESTY WORKOUT

Lead your students in an honesty workout designed to strengthen and define their truth muscles. Look over these suggestions, then adjust them to your class:

Workout Warm-ups

Warm-up for the honesty workout by leading your class in compiling in-depth data about ways people serve with honesty. Ask the following questions, then enter the responses onto a chart with approximately fifteen squares to the right of each entry. Each category of service, i.e., God, parents, teacher, should be on a separate piece of paper.

1. What actions would separate an honest follower of God from a dishonest follower?
2. How might a child give honest service to his/her parents?
3. In what ways might a student honestly serve a teacher?
4. What honesties might a friend use in serving friends honestly?
5. How might a citizen serve honestly?

The Workout

Using the information from each posterboard, do the following:

1. Instruct students to look for sightings of each of the data entries. Encourage scrutiny of the media, literature, home life, school, church, community.
2. When a sighting is made, the student places a check in the proper square and prepares to explain it to the class at a specified time.
3. Not the pattern of checks. Which boards are filling up most quickly? Why? Is it because these boards represent more easily noticed honesties or because people are more honest in those areas? Place a "1" next to the first entry to receive fifteen checks, a "2" next to the second entry, and so on.
4. Provide time for students to analyze their own levels of honesty in service. If desired, give each student an "honesty sheet" on which he/she notes personal progress and observations.

Warm-downs

Close the workout by evaluating the findings and coming to some intermediate conclusions about serving with honesty. If desired, ask a small team of students to condense the findings, photocopying the results for each student in your class and for others whom you feel would be interested.

HONESTY WORKOUT

PROJECT SERVANT

UNIT SIX: SENDING A MESSAGE THOROUGHLY

The group in the Servant Story were thorough in sending a message of love to all of the students in their school on Valentine's Day.

What message would your students like to send to their school, neighborhood, or community? How might they do it thoroughly? Pose these questions to them and let them take it from there.

Lead them through the suggestion stage, then help them settle on one as their choice. Use the activity as an opportunity for using skills learned elsewhere in the character study, such as orderly planning and meekness.

These five "d's" will help you develop (that's "D-velop"!) the plan:

1. Define the message.

The message: _____

2. Determine its recipients.

The recipients: _____

3. Design its form.

The form: _____

_____

4. Delegate its messengers.

The staff and their responsibilities: _____

_____

_____

_____

_____

5. Deliver it.

The details of the delivery: _____

_____

_____

_____

UNIT SEVEN: FRIENDLINESS

Lead your students into the world of friendship by implementing some of the following ideas:

1. FRIENDLY REPORTS

From a cup, students draw the name of one other student in your class. During a set amount of time, such as one week, the students will serve in a friendly manner the person whose name they have drawn. At the end of the period of time, the recipient of the friendliness writes a paragraph explaining the kinds of friendly service he/she has received.

2. FRIENDLINESS FORUM

Hold your own investigation of friendliness by using a panel of "experts," or by conducting your own Senate hearing on serving others with friendliness.

3. WHAT IS A FRIEND?

With your class, compose a composite of a friend. Encourage students to evaluate their own level of friendliness and to observe others who seem to be naturally friendly. Spend time evaluating the benefits of being friendly and considering the part friendliness plays in being a servant.

4. FRIENDLY FOCUS

With your class, select someone to receive focused friendliness from your class. Stress the idea of serving by being friendly. Apply the qualities from the composite in #3 in your service to (a) someone new to your school, (b) a person in your neighborhood or church, (c) a person living in another country, such as other believers who are serving God as missionaries.

PROJECT SERVANT

UNIT EIGHT: MEET GOD EXTRAVAGANZA!

The term "witness" often scares us. Actually, witnessing is simply telling another person about a product, activity, or person we are pleased with. Your students have learned many reasons to be pleased with God. This project will give them a comfortable, even fun, way of expressing their pride and admiration of God.

To prepare for this event, students will first gather information about God and then design ways to communicate that information to others. You are encouraged to follow these suggestions in planning your own MEET GOD EXTRAVAGANZA.

1. Determine as a class what kinds of things about God you want to tell the world. Choices may include: His words; His bold acts; His creativity; His good ideas; His plans for His children; His promises; His power; His love.

2. Select ways to present each category to those who will attend the event. Choices may include: Skits with or without costumes; colorful banners; slide or video presentations of pre-performed dramas or talk shows; brochures detailing reasons for trusting Him; baseball-card type hero stories showing how God has worked in people's lives; artistic renditions of Solomon's temple and student projections of life in Heaven; time lines; live or recorded music performed by your talented students; food fit for a King – Jesus!

3. Plan a time to present your MEET GOD EXTRAVAGANZA. Select guests and a way of inviting them.

4. Assign students to committees; enlist parent and administrative help. Committees may include: Program (with sub-committees for each event), Publicity, Room decorations, Food. Everyone cleans up.

5. Seek to promote the truth that God finds great pleasure in our praise and admirations of Him. Mention often that He is observing the plans and progress of the event and will be there on that special day, as He is everyday. Encourage students to think of ways to let God know that they are doing this for Him.

BACKFIRE!
A Melodrama based on the life of Queen Esther

The following melodrama is an effective wrap-up of the study of Queen Esther. You may wish to perform it for family and friends as a spring or end-of-year production, for fellow students as a chapel presentation, or simply as an in-class review.

It is intended to be a lively and entertaining, yet meaningful, activity, requiring minimal costuming. The following suggestions may help you in your planning:

Option: If you wish, you may choose to take slides ahead of time of the scenes mentioned in the narrators' dialogues. Then, as each part of the story is mentioned by the narrator, a set of slides would be shown.

Publicity: Ask one or two of your artistic students to design a program cover. Use that same design on all flyers and posters. Inside the program, list *all* actors and staging assistants, as well as any stores, parents, and friends who have helped you.

Costuming: Use common items, such as a tablecloth for Esther's veil or a colander for the king's crown.

Music: Organ or piano music for background and mood only, no singing accompaniment. Ask organist to imitate the old silent movie style of playing.

Scene changes: Mark scene changes by sending students across the stage with signs that name the location of the scene, i.e., "King's Courtyard."

Audience participation: The fun of a melodrama is the interplay between the actors and the audience. Encourage your actors to play to the audience, and print "Boo! Hiss!" and "Cheer!" on posterboards and have a student hold them up at appropriate moments. If desired, "plant" students in the audience to be leaders in booing and hissing and cheering.

Lights: Lighting tips are included in the script if you choose to use them.

Cast: King Xerxes
Queen Esther
Mordecai
Haman
Narrator – Chief Palace Guard
Narrator – Assistant Palace Guard
Haman's wife and friends
Reader
Guard with speaking part
Other guards
Messenger
Maidens (servants)
Clergyman

Remember: This is your class and your production. Take the basic script and suggestions and adjust them as simply or elaborately as you wish. Enjoy!

BACKFIRE!

SCRIPT

Spotlight on narrator. Other lights off.
Music playing softly as narrator speaks.

NARRATION (By Chief Palace Guard and his Assistant)

CHIEF Hello. As the chief palace guard . . .

ASSISTANT . . . and assistant chief palace guard . . .

CHIEF . . . during the reign of the mighty King Xerxes, we saw many unusual and exciting events. But none could compare to the one we will tell you about now.

ASSISTANT I agree.

CHIEF It centers around four people . . .

ASSISTANT Five really . . .

CHIEF . . . whose lives intertwined to form a most interesting pattern of adventure. Xerxes, an overly-generous king who loved showing off his wealth, had thrown an 180-day political party for the officials of Persia. He had ended it with a week-long banquet where he let his guests drink all of the wine they wished. Toward the end of the banquet, after Xerxes had shown off his other treasures, the king decided that he wanted Queen Vashti to appear before the men to display her beauty. Vashti refused to appear.

ASSISTANT But only because she knew that the king would want her to do . . . well . . . uh . . . certain embarrassing things in front of the men.

CHIEF This bold act shook the confidence of the king and his leaders. (Assistant is chuckling and slapping his knee remembering the sight.) In order to prevent other wives from following Vashti's example, the frightened men quickly made a new law saying that all wives must obey their husbands. To show the dangers of not obeying, Queen Vashti was de-throned and a search began to find her replacement.

ASSISTANT One candidate for queen was a girl named Esther. Oh, and a beauty she was!

CHIEF Esther's parents had died when she was a young child. Her cousin, Mordecai, a loyal and respected Jew who worked on the palace staff, adopted her and raised her as his own child. Of all the queen candidates, the eunuch in charge of the young beauties liked Esther the best. He made sure she had the finest of everything.

ASSISTANT The king agreed with the eunuch and he chose Esther to be his queen.

CHIEF (To assistant) I was getting to that!

ASSISTANT (To chief) Sorry! (Shrugs his shoulders and looks at audience with a grin.)

Spotlight off narrators.
Music changes to wedding music.

SCENE ONE
The Wedding

Lights up on stage.

King Xerxes is on the platform with a clergyman in a robe. Guards stand on either side of the aisle with swords raised and crossed at the tips. Esther walks down the aisle under the swords and up to the platform to meet Xerxes.

Conduct a simple ceremony, with attendants if desired.

Audience cheers at end of the ceremony. King and Queen walk back down the aisle through the audience.

Lights out on stage.

End of Scene One

Spotlight on narrators.

NARRATION

CHIEF   Shortly after the newlyweds were settled, King Xerxes made a startling announcement regarding a change in staff.

ASSISTANT   It startled me, all right! (Pause to look at chief.) And him, as I recall! (Grins at audience.)

CHIEF   (Not amused.) He had named Haman to be second in command. (BOO! HISS!) Haman loved collecting power. He was proud and conceited and able to tell lies in a way that made people believe him.

ASSISTANT   (To audience.) **I** never believed him.

CHIEF   Because he was second in command, everyone was to bow as he passed by. Everyone did, except for one palace person.

ASSISTANT   (Rubbing his hands together in delight.) Oooo, this is where it starts getting good.

Spotlight off narrators.
Lights up on stage at palace gate.

SCENE TWO
The Plot

(Mordecai and others are in the palace courtyard working at the palace gate.)

HAMAN   (Enters looking conceited and obviously expecting all to bow. All do bow except Mordecai.) (BOO! HISS!) Hello, everyone. Hello, hello, hello. (Notices Mordecai standing.) You there! Don't you know who I am?

MORDECAI   I do.

HAMAN   Then why are you not honoring me by bowing?

MORDECAI   Because I bow to no man. (CHEER!)

HAMAN   (To the audience.) We'll see about that! (Exits to another spot on the stage representing his room.) (BOO! HISS!)

Lights off stage.
Spotlight on Haman in his room.

HAMAN (Looking frustrated.) That is the eighth time Mordecai has refused to bow to me. If this continues, who knows what will happen. I can't put up with such embarrassment. What would the king think if he knew that a mere palace worker was not honoring me?

(Paces back and forth three times as if thinking. Each time, he stops suddenly, turns to audience and says, "I've got it!" and then, "No, that won't work.") (After last pace.) I've really got it this time. Yes, yes, I've got it. And just in time for my meeting with the King. Yippee! (BOO! HISS!)

(Leaps toward another section of the stage representing the King's Courtyard.)

After a few leaps, turn spotlight off.
Lights up on stage in king's courtyard.

KING (As if concluding a meeting with Haman.) Well, that's all I have to say. How are things going in your new position, Haman?

HAMAN Funny you should ask, Your Highness. There is something I feel you should know.

KING Oh? What is it?

HAMAN Well, Your Dearly Loved Highness, there is a group of people in your kingdom who keep to themselves and refuse to obey you. Now a man of your influence and stature should not be bothered with such folk. I suggest we get rid of them for you. I myself would be happy to do it. In fact, I will put in ten thousand of my own dollars to help it happen.

KING Keep your money, Haman. But do as you wish with the people. Here is my ring. Use it to seal the decree. (Yawns, stretches.) Anything else?

HAMAN No, Your Highness. That is quite enough.

KING Very well, then. Excuse me . . . (yawn) while I take a little snooze.

HAMAN Of course, Your Highness. Sleep well. (Haman waits with phony grin until the King exits, then he leaps up with one fist in the air.) Yeah! I'll show you, Mordecai. You and everyone like you! (BOO! HISS!)

Lights off.

End of Scene Two

Spotlight on narrators.

NARRATION

CHIEF Haman used the king's ring to sign a law that ordered all Jews to be killed on the sixteenth day of the month of Adar. When Mordecai heard about Haman's wicked law, he was overcome with grief. Weeping bitterly, Mordecai exchanged his everyday clothes for those made of sackcloth. He poured ashes on his head, showing everyone the extent of his sorrow.

ASSISTANT Yes, and when Esther heard about it, she was embarrassed. She sent a change of clothes out to him with a note telling him to put them on. But he wouldn't. And so, Esther . . .

CHIEF (Clearing his throat to interrupt.) Esther, knowing that something terrible must have happened to cause Mordecai to do this, sent him another note.

Lights off narrators.

SCENE THREE
The Decision

Lights up on stage. Scene will jump from palace gate to Esther's room.

MORDECAI (Mordecai stops wailing to read the note brought to him by messenger. He reads it out loud.) "What terrible thing has happened to you to cause you to wear sackcloth and ashes?" (Mordecai scribbles a note on the back of Esther's note and gives it to the messenger.)

ESTHER (Esther receives the note and reads it aloud.) "The wicked Haman has made a law signed with the king's ring to slaughter our people on the thirteenth of Adar. You must beg the king for mercy and plead with him for your people." (Esther shows shock and anger over Haman's plot, then writes another note and sends it with the messenger.)

MORDECAI (Mordecai reads the note out loud.) "You know that I can't just walk in to see the king without permission! No one can! The law states that those bothering the king will be put to death unless he raises his golden sceptor to them." (He again writes on the back of the note and returns it to Esther with the messenger.)

ESTHER (Esther reaches for the note eagerly when the messenger returns with it. Reads it out loud.) "Don't think that because you are the queen that your life will be spared by Haman. I believe our people will be delivered, if not by you then by some other way. But either way, your life and mine are in danger. Besides, who is to say that you were not made to be queen so that you could save your people?"

Spotlight on narrators.

NARRATION

CHIEF The queen was in turmoil over this decision. Should she risk her own life for her people by going in to the king unannounced? Or should she just do nothing and hope that no one would find out she was also a Jew?

ASSISTANT Of course, either way, she was in a whole lot of trouble!

CHIEF When she finally did make her decision, she sent word to Mordecai. He was hungry to know if his cousin would act with courage or if she would behave in a cowardly way.

Spotlight off narrators.

MORDECAI (Reads the note brought to him by the messenger.) "Gather our people together and fast for me. Don't eat or drink for three days, night or day. My maids and I will do the same. When the three days are up, I will go into the king even though it is against the law. And, if I die, I die." (CHEER!)

Lights out.

End of Scene Three

Spotlight on narrators.

NARRATION

CHIEF On the third day of the fast, Esther kept her promise to Mordecai and the people. She put on her finest garments and robes and walked to the king's court. At his door, she took a deep breath . . .

ASSISTANT A really deep breath . . .

CHIEF . . . and opened the door.

SCENE FOUR
The Banquet

Lights up on stage.

ESTHER	(Esther steps forward in king's court. He is sitting on his throne and looks up.) Excuse me, Your Highness.
KING	(Looks up and for a moment shows no movement. Then, with a grin, he picks up his sword and raises it to her. She touches its tip.) Esther! Welcome. What is it you want, my dear? I'll give you up to half of my kingdom.
ESTHER	(Speaks cautiously.) If it pleases the king, I would like you and Haman to come to a banquet I have prepared for you.
KING	(Looking jolly and excited about the idea of another party.) That sounds like a grand idea, Esther. We will be right there. (To the guard) Guards! Bring Haman to me. We're going to go to Esther's for dinner!

Lights out.
Spotlight on narrators.
Music plays "Tea for Two."

NARRATION

CHIEF	Haman was glad to hear about the invitation.
ASSISTANT	Of course he was. He liked anything that made him look important!
CHIEF	The two men ate a delicious meal with Esther. After dinner, the king sat back and asked the queen again what it was she really wanted.

Lights off narrators.
Lights up on stage.

KING	So now, Esther, I really must know what it is you want.
ESTHER	If you view me with favor, my king, and if it pleases you, let the king and Haman come tomorrow to another banquet I will prepare for you. Then I will tell you what it is that I want.
KING	Very well! We'll be delighted to repeat this wonderful idea! Won't we, Haman!"
HAMAN	Yes! Yes! We would!
CHIEF	Haman held in his screams of joy until he passed through the doors of his own house.
ASSISTANT	He was looking forward to another turn at feeling important.
HAMAN	(Runs through the door of his house, jumping and clapping, yelling.) You'll never guess what just happened! The queen just had the king and I to dinner. Just us! No one else! (Stops for a breath.) And guess what again! She has invited me back for another banquet tomorrow! (Leaps proudly.) She must finally realize how special I really am! (BOO! HISS!) (Mood changes suddenly. He becomes sullen and angry.) But the truth is, none of these good things really matter to me as long as that awful Mordecai refuses to honor me by bowing to me.
HAMAN'S WIFE	Good grief, Haman! Just build high gallows for the man and hang him. Get the king's permission first thing in the morning and hang Mordecai before lunch. Then go and enjoy your little banquet with the king and queen!

HAMAN	Brilliant idea, dear! I'll do it! I will, I will!

End of Scene Four

Lights out on stage.

SCENE FIVE
The Honor

Spotlight on narrators.

NARRATION

CHIEF	The king's curiosity kept him from sleeping well that night. When he ran out of ideas about Esther's request and was still not asleep, Xerxes woke up his servants and told them to read him the history books.
ASSISTANT	He was sure history would put him to sleep.
CHIEF	But he was wrong. Instead, he was wide awake when he heard about a plot to kill the king.
ASSISTANT	A plot that **Mordecai** had uncovered!
KING	I was getting to that!
ASSISTANT	Oh. Sorry. (Shrugs to audience.)

Lights off narrators.
Lights up on stage in king's room.

KING	Has that man Mordecai been rewarded for his loyalty to me?
READER	No, Your Highness. Nothing has been done for him.

Lights off stage and on narrators.

CHIEF	In the meantime, Haman couldn't wait to hang Mordecai, so he went to the palace at dawn to ask permission to hang him. When the king heard someone in the courtyard, he asked who it was.
ASSISTANT	When he heard that it was Haman, he invited him in.

Lights off narrators.
Lights up on stage.

HAMAN	(BOO! HISS!) Yes, Your Highness? How can I help the king?
KING	Tell me, Haman, what should I do for someone I want to honor?
HAMAN	(Taking a deep breath and "puffing up" while looking at audience, pointing to self as if knowing that the king was wanting to honor **him.**) Well, let me see, Your Highness. I know! I know! First, I would place one of the king's own robes and crowns on the man. Then I would place him on one of the king's own horses – one with a crest on it – and march him through the streets with one of the king's most trusted servants yelling, "This is the one whom the king wants to honor!"
KING	Excellent idea! No wonder I made you second in command of the kingdom. You have good ideas! Now, I want you to be in charge of doing exactly as you have said to the man Mordecai as a reward for the loyalty he has shown me. (CHEER!)
HAMAN	(Looking deflated and shocked, but not wanting the king to notice. Speaks and walks weakly.) Yes, Your Highness. Anything you say.

KING	Well, hurry up! I want it done this morning. (Haman exits.)

Lights off stage.
Spotlight on narrators.

CHIEF	Somehow, Haman managed to carry out the orders of the King. He led Mordecai through the streets of the town giving honor to the man he hated. When it was over, he rushed home . . .
ASSISTANT	. . . to cry on the shoulders of his family and friends.

Lights off narrators and on stage at Haman's house.

HAMAN	(Enters his home and flings himself on a chair, moaning.) Oh, no! You won't believe what kind of day I have had. The king found some old page in history that said Mordecai had uncovered a plot to assassinate him. He gave me the "honor" of marching him through town on the king's own horse.
HAMAN'S WIFE	(Shaking her head and speaking unsympathetically.) It is obvious that Mordecai has started your downfall, Haman. On top of that, he is a Jew. There is no way you will stand against him.

Spotlight on narrators.

CHIEF	Even in their foolishness, Haman's wife and friends were wise enough to know that the God of Israel is more powerful than anyone's wicked schemes. Before anyone could say another word, the king's servants came to take Haman to Esther's next banquet.

Spotlight off narrators.
Lights up on stage.

End of Scene Five

SCENE SIX
The Backfire

Spotlight on narrators.

CHIEF	The ride to the palace was too short for Haman. He needed more time to get himself ready to pretend everything was all right.
HAMAN	(In a whiny, helpless voice to himself.) How can I sit at a dinner with Xerxes and Esther knowing that Mordecai has just made a fool out of me in front of the entire city! (BOO! HISS!)
CHIEF	When Haman finally arrived, he and the impatient king hurried down to Esther's banquet hall and began eating.
ASSISTANT	Not that anyone tasted the food. Their minds were telling them other things. And finally, when dinner was over . . . (Chief Narrator interrupts with a nudge.)
CHIEF	(Clears throat.) When dinner was over, the king again asked Esther what it was that she wanted from him. He reminded her that she could ask for anything up to half of the kingdom.
ESTHER	(Choosing words carefully.) If I have found favor with the king, and if it pleases your majesty, I plead for my life and the life of my people.
KING	(Looking shocked and sitting up.) What do you mean? Why are you and your people in danger?
HAMAN	(Coughs and moves to the edge of his seat in shock.)

ESTHER	I and my people have been sold to be slaughtered. (Her voice is growing louder, yet is still under control.)
KING	(Standing up and planting himself in front of her.) Who has dared to sell your people, Esther? Tell me! I want to know!
HAMAN	(Wiping his brow and shaking. Doesn't know whether to stand or sit.) (To audience in a loud whisper.) Esther is a Jew?!
ESTHER	The man who wants me and my people destroyed is this vile Haman!
KING	What? Haman has done this dreadful thing to you? (To Haman.) You . . . you . . . despicable rat . . . (leaves room quickly to go to garden.)
HAMAN	(Sees Esther as his only hope and throws himself across her lap as the king returns to the room.) Please, Esther, save me. He is going to kill me. Please! I didn't mean it!
KING	(Re-enters room and points at Haman, yelling his words.) So, it isn't enough that you try to kill the queen, now you are trying to molest her, too!
HAMAN	No! No! That isn't it. I swear, it isn't. Your Highness, have mercy on me . . .
KING	Guards! Take him away and kill him!
GUARD	Your Highness. Haman has built tall gallows for Mordecai.
KING	Good! Use them for Haman. (CHEER!) (Guards drag Haman away down aisle through audience, King walks toward Esther to comfort her.)

Lights off.
Spotlight on narrators.

NARRATION

CHIEF	That day Haman was hung from the gallows he had built for Mordecai. The king gave Haman's estate to Esther, who put Mordecai in charge of it. The king also gave Haman's job to Mordecai and gave him the ring Haman had used to seal the deadly decree.
ASSISTANT	Esther and Mordecai were given permission to write another decree giving the Jews permission to defend themselves against their attackers on the thirteenth of Adar. And that is what they did.
CHIEF	The day was named "Purim," because Haman had cast lots, or Pur, to choose the day of slaughter. Every year, the Jews celebrate Purim by feasting and giving gifts to one another.
ASSISTANT	And so ends the story of history's loudest backfire.
CHIEF	I was going to say that.
ASSISTANT	(Grinning broadly.) It **was** a good line, wasn't it. (To audience.) Goodbye!

Spotlight off narrators.
Lights up on stage.

THE END

ALL PARTICIPANTS TAKE BOWS IN THIS ORDER:
Guards, Reader, Haman's wife and friends, Chief Narrator, Assistant Narrator, Mordecai, King Xerxes, Haman, and Esther. (Boo, Hiss, and cheer appropriately.)